My Journey in Overcoming Chronic Dysthymic Depression

My Journey in Overcoming Chronic Dysthymic Depression

Patricia Adrian Jordan

CrossBooks™
A Division of LifeWay
1663 Liberty Drive
Bloomington, IN 47403
www.crossbooks.com
Phone: 1-866-879-0502

© 2013 Patricia Adrian Jordan. All rights reserved.

No part of this book may be reproduced, stored in a retrieval system, or transmitted by any means without the written permission of the author.

First published by CrossBooks 3/25/2013

ISBN: 978-1-4627-2566-3 (sc)
ISBN: 978-1-4627-2568-7 (hc)
ISBN: 978-1-4627-2567-0 (e)
Library of Congress Control Number: 2013903869

Printed in the United States of America

This book is printed on acid-free paper.

Any people depicted in stock imagery provided by Thinkstock are models, and such images are being used for illustrative purposes only.

Certain stock imagery © Thinkstock.

Scripture taken from the New King James Version. Copyright 1979, 1980, 1982 by Thomas Nelson, inc. Used by permission. All rights reserved.

Scripture quotations taken from the New American Standard Bible®, Copyright © 1960, 1962, 1963, 1968, 1971, 1972, 1973, 1975, 1977, 1995 by The Lockman Foundation. Used by permission." (www.Lockman.org)

Because of the dynamic nature of the Internet, any web addresses or links contained in this book may have changed since publication and may no longer be valid. The views expressed in this work are solely those of the author and do not necessarily reflect the views of the publisher, and the publisher hereby disclaims any responsibility for them.

Do not rejoice over me, my enemies.
Though I fall I will rise;
Though I dwell in darkness, the
Lord is a Light for me.
(Micah 7:8 New American Standard)

A Note about My Chapters

I arranged my short chapters chronologically, as it has happened. Most chapters are only one page long, but a few are longer. I did this partly because it is a writing style that seems natural to me, but also I felt it was the best way to emphasize what I wanted to say about that particular issue in my life. More important, though, brief chapters are the best way to emphasize my healing from mental and emotional issues that have controlled my life for far too long.

I hope that in reading my story you will experience a deeper, more enriched peace on your life's journey.

Contents

Preface xiii
Acknowledgments xv
Introduction xvii
I'm Both Healed and Being Healed of Depression 1
From Journaling to Writing My Story 2
The Power of Myths 3
My Earliest Memory 4
My Father: Myron Grayson (M. G.) Bell 5
My Mother: June Lloyd Bell 6
A Day Visit to My Grandparents' House in Murphy 7
Does Depression Start in Infancy? 9
My Parents Clashed 10
Not Making Things Right 12
Overcoming Stuttering 13
Childhood: Shaping vs. Breaking? 15
Stinking Thinking 16
Blue Days 18
The Beginnings of My Christian Faith 19

Happy Childhood Memories 20
Cherokee, North Carolina, and Achieving the American Dream 21
The Birth of Cherokee Sales Company Inc. 23
Cherokee Sales Company Incorporated 24
The Original Hillbilly Calendar 28
My Angry, Loving, Caring Parents 30
My Mom Became a Victor 32
Being Raised to Live in Fear 33
Aimlessness and Depression Are Related 36
A Life-Saving Miracle Phone Call 37
Life-Changing Events 39
Rekindling My Love for Christ 41
Moving to Spangdahlem Air Base, Germany 43
"Lucky" and Marlene Lyons' Den 45
God Created Marriage—We Add the Joy! 47
My Very Difficult In-Laws 49
Forgiving Difficult Relatives! 52
What Do We Do with Our Anger? 53
Trademarks We're Known By 55
Both of Our Attitudes Needed Changing 56
Benefits of Successful Counseling 57
Taking Ownership of My Issues 79
My Emotional Healing 81

How I Learned to Avoid, Deny, and Enable 82
The Importance of Acceptance and Validation 83
Shifting My Paradigm from Victim to Victor 85
Solving My ADD 87
Attention Deficit Disorder in My Family 89
My Daughter Was Diagnosed with ADD 90
The Importance of Positive Healing Messages 92
Moving to Western North Carolina 94
Deep Sleep Test 96
Closure 97
What Are the Signs of Depression? 98
Personality Disorder 99
Personality Disorders Do Exist 101
Accept the Truth 102
My Reality Needed Changing 103
Meridian Counseling Center 105
Seeking Truth Brings Peace 107
4 Fs 109
Unexpected Closure for Me 111
Solutions to Loving Difficult People 113
Improving My Physical Health and Managing RA 114
The Valley of Trouble, the Door of Hope 117
The Door, the Key 118
Boundaries by Drs. Townsend and Cloud 119

What I've Learned through Counseling and My Own Seeking 120

A Vision God Gave to Me 127

Your Miracle Is at Hand! 128

Some Laws Should Never Be Broken 130

Watch Out for the Trapdoor! 131

Three Different Time Zones 132

Contact the Author 135

Preface

I've never seen myself as a writer; I'm surprised I've even kept up with my journaling! However, when I caught a vision of others suffering from dysthymic depression, like I have, or depression worse than mine, I knew I needed to write about my own victory in overcoming chronic low-grade depression. I dedicate my book to those who are earnestly seeking freedom from any kind of emotional turmoil.

I did not write my book with any guile or underhanded thoughts motivating me. As much as possible, I've let the key players in my life know that I have written this book and have invited each one to read any part or all of it. I've been open minded to receiving correction where needed. I have a clear heart and conscious on every event I've written about. I simply hope my story will minister to you as much as it has ministered to and freed me in writing it.

When I started writing, I was not on a mission to write a book, which freed me to relax and, through free association, explore my experiences from my most painful to my most wonderful. I simply wrote and wrote and wrote, and then I started feeling even better than I could have imagined! Through this cathartic experience, I realized I had written a self-help book without planning to. I hope my efforts aid you in your healing. *Shalom*, friend!

Acknowledgments

I thank the Lord Jesus Christ for my many blessings.

A big thank you goes to my husband, Jeff; our three daughters, Ruth, Rachel, and Esther; and to my extended family for their love, support, and willingness to listen—to simply listen. Least only in size is my pet miniature poodle, Skeeter, who for more than a decade now has protected me and made sure that he and I get out for our daily walks.

A special thank you goes to the team at Meridian Behavioral Health Center for teaching me how to move those emotional "boulders" off my path! It was your teamwork that placed me securely on my healing journey.

Grateful appreciation goes out to my family in Christ at Grace Community Church and especially to Dr. (Reverend) Richard "Rich" Peoples. You all have given more to me than any of you will ever know.

Introduction

In April of 2008, I was correctly diagnosed with dysthymic depression. Finally, I had found a therapist who correctly put her finger on my exact problem. Dysthymic depression is described as a lingering malaise about nothing specific, just life in general. For me, it was living life while being in a mental mist or haze. Decisions seemed to endlessly be put on a back burner, and just leaving my house seemed like it required breaking gravitational force! I've spent huge amounts of my life distressing over the small impacts of life.

I'm still in love with the man I married over three decades ago, and we have raised three daughters of whom I'm very proud of. Life has treated me fairly, yet also painfully unfairly as well. It's how I've adjusted to and sought help with the unfair parts that really makes for the whole of my book.

Am I healed? Well, I'm certainly more aware of what causes my deeper slumps and have learned to avoid those dark pits. Professional counseling, herbal remedies, and of course, a healthy lifestyle have all helped. I have included in these pages what I've learned and am continuing to learn.

I was molded to be a "fixer." However, through my intense searching for peace and methods for best working through life's stressors, I am living one day at a time, recasting my self-image for my own benefit. I hope that what I've learned and have written about will help you as well.

I'm Both Healed and Being Healed of Depression

This isn't a book on the latest therapy ideas. Nor is it a book of homespun advice. I don't hand out advice to my adult children—they would barely listen to it anyway—and I've stayed true to my nature here as well.

I am also not trying to get pity by writing about my life. Pity doesn't help or heal. It doesn't change anything for the good. My book is about the healthy ways I've found to let go of negative emotions that can block anyone's healing and how I replaced them with healthy emotions of forgiveness and love.

I am a Christian and have mentioned my faith where I feel it appropriate to do so. "I am not ashamed of the gospel" (Rom. 1:16a NAS).

The journaling I did that snowballed into this book has helped me to release many pent-up negative emotions that I was not consciously aware I had even after I had gone through quite a bit of therapy. I'm continually finding healthy paths to travel on, so I can truly say I'm both healed of and am continually being healed of depression.

From Journaling to Writing My Story

On December 4, 2009, my eighty-three-year-old mother passed away. In the following January, while I was having corrective foot surgery, I "visited" my mother. I floated in a fog and could not see her, but I knew I was in my mother's presence. She talked to me at length, but I have never been able to recall exactly what she said. Nevertheless, after surgery the first thing I said to my daughter Esther who was with me was, "I just visited my mom!"

I do believe my mother gave me her blessing to write my story. Her knowledge is now complete because she is in the presence of Jesus, no longer limited to earthly understanding. "For now we see in a mirror dimly, but then face to face; now I know in part, but then I will know fully just as I have also been fully known" (1 Cor. 13:12 NAS).

While I was convalescing—and also mourning—I began journaling, but I didn't have a goal of writing a book then. I had to "grow into those shoes"! Either snatches of generational accounts came into my consciousness or my relatives shared a more complete account of an event that has been woven into the following short stories. I learned the details of many things, both good and bad, when I visited my mother at her home while she was living.

When I did start to write, I brushed up on Windows and Word by calling my oldest daughter Ruth to ask how to write and save to file so I could easily locate my story whenever the inspiration hit me. My husband, Jeff, helped me a lot by finishing all the room painting projects I was in the middle of while he was convalescing from atrial fibrillation during 2011. I'm grateful to everyone who helped me so I could finish this project.

The Power of Myths

We all have heard or read mythological tales. Parts of each tale are perhaps based on tidbits of factual events, and then fantasy weaves itself around those droplets of truth and a myth is formed. Sometimes it's hard to tell where the truth ends and mistruths begin.

Often, bits of truth become interwoven with harmful myths that weave their way into our personal beliefs. This is a part of what my book is about—how I finally began to separate the truth from the fiction of what I had heard about myself and what I eventually came to believe about myself that was truth after weeding out what wasn't!

During my most important formative years (preadolescence), I frequently heard a series of negative statements about myself that I began to believe were true. My parents believed in the negative myths, or at least they kept repeating them to me as well as to others. The problem, though, was that each myth was based on their opinions and not the truth.

As I grew older, I based many of my decisions about my life around or upon those mistruths about me. My parents, who first spoke the myths to me—actually, about me in my presence—never told me that their myths were all based on personal opinion and not necessarily truth. Unfortunately, each myth was harmful to me. Over a long period of time, their, and others', angry words nearly destroyed me.

How I Overcame Dysthymic Depression is actually about the unraveling of those myths, which has taken me through the valley of the shadow (Ps. 23:4) and into good, solid mental and emotional health. It has been a long time in coming, but thank God I have arrived!

My Earliest Memory

My earliest memory is a brief one of my dad holding out shiny keys for me to toddle across the living room to. My mom was holding me steady while my grandparents, along with my older siblings, were coaxing me on. We were at my grandparents' home in Murphy, North Carolina.

I was born in Murphy on May 5, 1952. I'm the youngest of five children. We came along pretty quickly after my parents were married—there are just six years between my oldest sibling and myself. Likely, my parents didn't plan for us to be that close in age; maybe they didn't even plan how many children they wanted. However, both of them worked hard to take care of our physical needs. Even with all of their efforts, though, even in their most senior years, they still remember local churches sometimes leaving food baskets on our doorstep during those early years.

They did experience at least one miracle while we lived there. My brother David was born very anemic. The doctor didn't give my parents much hope that he would live but did arrange for an appointment as soon as possible with the only pediatrician in all of western North Carolina for Mom and tiny, underweight David. The pediatrician's office was about fifty miles away, in Sylva.

All through David's first year, my strong-willed mother determinedly took him on that once-a-week Greyhound bus ride to the pediatrician's office. The trip from Murphy to Sylva was a long one that started early in the morning and ended late in the day for the two of them.

After his first touch-and-go year, David pulled through and strengthened enough to become regular height and weight. As an adult, he has been the fire chief for the nearby rural community of Whittier for more than two decades.

My Father: Myron Grayson (M. G.) Bell

My dad was born on October 24, 1924, the third child of four that were born to Clyde and Etta (Jones) Bell. He grew up in Knoxville, Tennessee. When my dad was thirteen years old, his dad died suddenly of a massive heart attack. This tragedy must've hit my dad extra hard because he was Clyde's favorite one out of the four. Monday through Friday Clyde had worked on the railroad, but on Saturdays he took my dad who was just entering his preteen years during that time, and taught him the fine art of selling by approaching local merchants to buy calendar space on the next year's issue.

I believe my dad bottled up his grief over his dad's death, and that's what fueled his anger that came out much later on when he became my father. I've read in several of my healing books that unresolved grief often turns to anger years and years later on.

About a year later, Dad dropped out of school during his ninth-grade year. For most of his teen years, Dad found it hard to stay in one place for very long. He rode railcars or hitched rides and traveled all over the Southeast, but he seemed to always end up right back where he had started, in Knoxville. When WWII started, he joined the Marine Corps and was stationed in Newfoundland, Canada. Dad was assigned to a supply unit, and that steady routine enabled him to complete his GED, an accomplishment that made his mother happy. After his enlistment was up, he went back to Knoxville, where he met my mother.

My Mother: June Lloyd Bell

My mother was born on May 17, 1926, in Murphy, North Carolina. She also was the third child of four born to my grandparents, Dewey and Myrtle (Johnson) Lloyd. Mom grew up in Murphy, which was then and still is a small town in western North Carolina.

Mom always put her best efforts into whatever she did, finishing high school as an honor grad. Right after graduating, she and her younger sister, Mary Jo, who had graduated at the same time, (my mom chose to start school late so she and Aunt Mary Jo could attend school together) rode a train down to Pensacola, Florida where they joined their parents. Mom and my Aunt Mary Jo had spent their last year of high school somewhat being on their own because their parents had temporarily moved to Pensacola to work on the huge naval base there. My grandparents fortunately had lots of *kinfolk* in Murphy the girls could count on if they needed help.

America was deeply involved in WWII at that time, and it was common for Americans to relocate to help in the war effort. For about that next year, my mom and my aunt were gun turret welders. They were assigned that job because they were petite, agile, and quick to learn (their lifetime blessings).

After they all returned to Murphy, Mom and Aunt Mary Jo moved to Knoxville, Tennessee, where they attended Knoxville Business School. Mom worked part-time at a theater and met Dad by selling him his nightly movie ticket. Shortly after she graduated they married.

A Day Visit to My Grandparents' House in Murphy

I have many warm memories of being in my maternal grandparents' old white, one-story farmhouse that sits right at the edge of Murphy. I believe I spent my first couple of Christmases there. I still have a vague memory of at least one of those times.

Whenever possible, as I pass through Murphy, I leave flowers on their graves or stop by the old house. I believe it's important to honor the good seed that has been sown into me.

The old house isn't lived in anymore but is still being used and kept up by the current owners. That's a testament to all the loving care that, primarily, my grandpa put into maintaining it. He was a painter by trade and traded work with a carpenter if something big needed fixing. Even in my childhood, he bartered his labor. If he loaned a tool out, he expected it back and sometimes even went and got it back. If he borrowed a tool, he was quick to return it after he put it in better shape than when he had gotten it!

Whenever my parents took us five kids to visit our grandparents, we always had a big dinner. Sometimes Aunt Mary Jo and her family from Knoxville came for the day, or my Uncle J.D. and his family came in from Elizabeth City for a week's visit.

One way my grandparents showed their love for us was by making sure we always ate well in their house. Granny's big dinners always included fried chicken that came from their chicken coop. At least once, we got there in time to see Grandpa kill the unlucky bird, which is still not a pleasant memory for me. I can still describe the headless-chicken-jerking scene with plenty of clarity.

When we went for dinner, we always got there in time for Mom and my sisters to help with the cooking. Mom usually bought a freshly baked bone-in ham, and Granny would already have corn cut off the cob ready to make into the best creamiest cream corn I've ever tasted. Then, she filled a baking sheet with hand-shaped biscuits and made a bowl of steaming hot milk gravy to go along with them. We would have a pot full of what Granny called "a'rish pataters," either mashed or boiled. Sometimes we also had a plate full of deviled "aggs"!

When we visited in the wintertime, she served us a big pot of "leather britches." These were pole beans that she had pierced with a needle and threaded, making big long strings of them. In late summer, Granny would hang the strings of beans on her screened-in back porch to dry. In the winter, she would unstring them, place them in a pot of water with a slice of cured side meat, and boil them down. They tasted really good!

During the summer, if we grandkids had picked blackberries before dinner, Granny would make a deep-dish cobbler for our dessert—our reward for not getting underfoot. Otherwise, because of Mom and her efforts, we would have an array of homemade pies or Granny's "stacked cake" to make sure we were completely satisfied at her table. Home-cooked goodness always drifted through the old farmhouse.

My maternal grandparents, the Lloyds, and my paternal grandmother, Etta Bell, made a lasting impression on my life, mostly because of the transparent honesty and affectionate love they showed to not only me but to all their grandchildren.

Does Depression Start in Infancy?

Bonding and nurturing are two investments in a child's life for which the rewards are not immediately seen. That fact made it hard for either of my parents to understand the importance of those two wonderful childhood ingredients. None of us could have verbalized to either of our parents that we were starving for a healthy show of affection or positive comment. It was always easier for them to criticize us or ignore us.

Instead of holding and rocking any of her five babies to sleep, Mom placed each of us in a crib in a back room, rolled us up in a blanket, and positioned a bottle in our mouths while she cleaned or cooked. As she told me, little nurturing was involved.

My oldest brother told me that he would often sneak into the bedroom where I was sucking my bottle, grab it, and run outside, throwing my bottle out into the yard and leaving me crying. Fortunately, we lived near my maternal grandparents for my first year, and it was Granny who kept us during the day and gave us plenty of affection. I believe that brief year of positive touch helped me to subconsciously form my enduring positive attitude regarding my own life.

My Parents Clashed

My parents certainly had their clashes. I remember Mom slinging a large cast-iron frying pan at Dad, and narrowly missing him, in our old house in West Asheville. My sister Deena remembers that incident better than I do and has told me that it started because Dad had been at home with us five kids all that day yet hadn't made even the simplest of suppers for us, while Mom had spent her day on her feet, working at Rose's Five and Dime. Dad has always known, at least during his adult years, how to cook simple meals; in my childhood, he fried us pork skins and once made us tamales, wrapping them in corn husks before frying them. I remember those, and they were delicious!

Dad has never liked much authority over him, or much routine or structure either. Mom, on the other hand, liked structure and routine; that's what kept her world in order, along with a freshly made pot of coffee and a pack of Pall Malls. Once she had those two items, then things got accomplished.

We could always count on a hot meal being ready within thirty or forty minutes of her walking in the door from work. It was her impersonal but steady, efficient routine that I created my fear-based sense of security in; nevertheless, it was a solid enough security that it has kept me from falling apart during some very high-stress times in my life.

Dad has never been the rigid black-and-white thinker that Mom was. He has been both oddly blessed and cursed with a multilayered Jekyll and Hyde personality. At home he could fill the air with his criticisms of whoever wasn't his favorite at the moment, but in public he proved to be very amiable and blessed with the gift of gab.

My best early childhood memories of Dad are those of when

he occasionally played Monopoly or softball with us kids on weekends. And during the summers, he hand-cranked buckets of delicious soft ice cream for us. A real treat, though, was when my parents took us to the Biltmore Dairy Bar, where we got ice cream cones that were as big as our heads!

Saturdays meant all of us piling in the car and traveling to the A & P grocery store over in Asheville. By this time, we had moved to the rural community of Fairview some ten miles away. My parents never left us at home on Saturdays, but they did leave us in the car while they shopped for groceries, at least a few times. My sister remembers that they repeatedly found four of us bruised and crying while one of our brothers randomly punched us in a vain attempt at getting us to stop crying. Eventually, they did give in to clear logic and took us inside with them.

Not Making Things Right

While we lived in Asheville, Dad sold restaurant equipment all over western North Carolina and did well at it, too. He is by nature a workaholic and a natural at sales. Mom and us kids usually ate supper without him except on the weekends. Dad let a lot of the burden of parenting fall to my mom and hated being bothered by us by the time he got home.

When my mother worked at Rose's Five and Dime at the Westgate Shopping Center, they made an adequate income, but she knew job advancements were limited. By the time I started school, we had moved to Fairview and lived on Garren Creek. Mom started working at a small factory nearby called C. P. Clare, where within a short while she was made a line supervisor.

Our daily routine by that time started with my oldest sister, Carol, who was maybe twelve by then, waking us kids up for school. Five days a week, she fixed hot cereal for four of us and fried an egg for my oldest brother Gene. Then, she made sure we were all ready for the school bus on time.

After school and during the summers, we girls cleaned house and did laundry. Carol and Deena even started supper before Mom got home. A lot of responsibility was placed on my sisters very early in their lives.

By the time Mom got home from work, I would often run to her to show any new bruises my brothers had given me, crying and hoping she would make things right. It took therapy that would come much later in my life to understand why neither of my parents ever attempted to make things right for me or my siblings.

Overcoming Stuttering

In my early childhood I stuttered. This anxiety tic irritated my parents so strongly that neither of them liked for me to speak directly to them.

During those years, I usually communicated to my two older sisters, Carol and Deena, what my needs or wants were by way of hand signals and halting speech. I thank God for both of my sisters being there for me during my childhood; we three are still close today.

When we moved to the rural community of Fairview, the five of us attended Fairview Elementary School. My third-grade teacher there was a very kind and gentle older woman named Mrs. Allison who was completely white-headed the year I had her as my teacher. Through her many years of teaching, she had become a very wise and giving teacher, and she proved to be a true godsend for me by single-handedly changing my speech pattern. I don't recall ever going to any special speech class; back in the early sixties, Fairview probably didn't even have a speech therapist.

It took Mrs. Allison all that school year, but she finally did get me to stop stuttering. I don't remember every technique she used with me, but I clearly remember one she used often, and that was during reading time. Naturally, I hated reading out loud; nevertheless, when my time came, I had to read out loud just like all the other kids had to.

During my reading time, Mrs. Allison would stand at my side resting one of her aged hands across my shoulder while, with her other hand, she pointed to each word. I had to clearly pronounce each word as she coaxed me along with calming words of assurance. That's all the speech therapy I can ever remember having. And it worked, that was the end of my stuttering!

My parents had my tonsils taken out the following summer because I had strep throat frequently that school year. After I got home from the surgery, they had a blue girls' bike waiting for me! Also, I remember Mrs. Allison visiting my family to see how I was doing. We all sat out in the front yard, and I clearly remember her letting me sit on her lap during her visit.

Childhood: Shaping vs. Breaking?

A childhood should be more about forging the good emotional and mental health of a future adult than having a child suffer through having her or his budding personality crushed by others' criticisms and constant and prolonged ignoring, neglecting, or outright physical abuse. I especially wish the last one wasn't true for anyone.

Everyone has different breaking points indicating the limits of what their psyches can handle. I can't compare my limits to yours; all I can do is to simply write about my own experiences and let you relate to them or not. But I am not condemning my parents. I want to make that perfectly clear. I believe that each of my parents acted somewhat ignorantly when they acted out their own unresolved anger that neither had dealt with correctly in their lives.

I believe that both of my parents, along with my brothers, on occasion pushed me to my breaking point during my childhood with both verbal and physical abuse. When I cried, I was whipped; when I was whipped, I cried. Eventually the crying got whipped out of me. Instead of focusing on this, I try to meditate on good family memories and happy childhood experiences.

Nevertheless, I know I didn't have the worst childhood possible; however, as I've already stated, everyone has different breaking points. I probably wouldn't have lasted very long growing up in some of my relatives' homes. We have one cousin who remembers begging my mom to let her stay with us and not send her back to her parents' home after spending just a few days at our house. I guess I never knew how lucky I actually was until I heard that one.

Stinking Thinking

I believe that early physical and verbal abuse by my parents as well as my brothers preconditioned me to having long periods of sadness and unfocused thinking. I've learned to call it victim thinking, though some call it stinking thinking. Through therapy, I have worked at breaking the cycle of stinking thinking in my life.

In my early childhood, Mom frequently carried me on her hip to prevent my brothers from bullying me; even with that, though, they sometimes succeeded. If Dad was called in later to "keep the peace," then he came out swinging with his forty-inch-long, one-inch-wide belt, then the aggressor and the victim both got plenty. Mom also used this style of disciplining. I clearly remember her chasing me down the hallway or pulling me out from under a bed so she could lay Dad's belt to my legs if one of my brothers had agitated me had I dared to defend myself.

I was never able to send an effective message to either of my brothers that they were not to bother me. They were both angry growing up, and when they saw me, they saw an easy target for their anger. I've always been much smaller than anyone else in my family; even as an adult, I'm four feet and ten inches tall. I believe the most significant reason behind their bullying us girls was the lack of respect my parents showed for my sisters and me.

Once during the summer, an argument erupted between one of my brothers and my sister Carol. He took a swing at her, and she slammed the kitchen door on him so quickly that he ended up shoving his fist through the back door glass. Blood went everywhere! We called mom at C. P. Clare and told her to come home quickly. Amazingly, my brother had only surface cuts. Mom, though, was sure mad about leaving her job early, and she pretty much just wanted to know why our brother had gotten upset. That sums up both Mom and Dad's odd child-rearing logic.

Dad has always had a more dominating personality than Mom, so his poor attitude toward females set the tone in our home. Where did he get his paradigm of womanhood? I believe he developed it subconsciously in his childhood because his mother was the only disciplinarian during his formative years, and he has always hated most of any authority that's ever been placed over him.

My mother had a backbone of steel and could handle a lot of stress. Even she had her breaking points, though. Their marriage was apparently often filled with stress. I remember hearing Mom vomiting in the bathroom either late at night or in the early morning hours. At times, she lived off of high-powered aspirin, coffee, and Pall Mall unfiltered cigarettes.

Actually, most of the time, we five kids got along fairly well when left to ourselves. After I got my bike, Gene would get the rest of us motivated for Sunday afternoon bike rides on rural, winding Garren Creek Road, or David and I would play for hours in the dirt with beat-up Matchbox cars.

Blue Days

I don't know exactly when I began having "blue days." Melancholy depression seems to have crept in too early for me to have been aware of it. I believe my parents just accepted it as part of my personality without realizing that they caused some of it. Perhaps they just put their heads in the sand and thought I would just grow out of it.

Neither of my parents encouraged, guided, or connected with me, and I was not raised too differently than my siblings were. It has taken therapy for me to connect to my grandchildren as much as I wish I had connected to my own children. Better late than never, but at least I was not as harsh to my own children in their rearing as my parents were to me in my childhood. I've come to understand and to believe how important positive touch is to the nurturing process of a young child. When my grandkids were younger and spent the night with me, I gave them a bath, wrapped each one in a towel, and gave them a big hug as a "finishing touch."

I'm not the therapist. I'm not trying to make a therapist statement when I hash over what went wrong in my childhood. Part of any healing is revisiting what went wrong in order to have closure and to be able to move onward with life today. I'm simply stating as much as possible the knowledge that I've learned through my own healing journey, hoping that by doing so I will continue my healing while I'm helping others in theirs.

The Beginnings of My Christian Faith

Both of my parents have always had faith in God, as did each of their parents. When we lived in Fairview, Sunday mornings meant listening to the WLOS TV Sunday morning gospel music hour. I remember the programs being live performances of musicians who were glad they had a chance to stop in Asheville to sing a few songs. By then, I was usually sitting on the couch smearing Vaseline on my scuffed-up patent-leather shoes, which instantly gave them a new look. Dad would often play his organ along with the singers. He was a self-taught organist who eventually learned to read sheet music.

We were in the habit of regular church attendance by the time we moved to Fairview. My parents joined the Fairview Baptist Church, which had a sanctuary built from quarried rock. I became a Christian at that church when I was very young. The minister would often accompany the Sunday night sermon with beautiful charcoal drawings of scenes from the Bible. He would turn his easel toward us while he sat at an angle so that we were able to watch him fill a large sheet of paper with vibrant colors, beautifully drawing biblical scenes. I'm a visual learner, and those wordless sermons spoke volumes to me. My sisters and I were baptized in that church.

Neither of my brothers cared for church, so within a few years those peaceful Sunday mornings were often filled with one of them yelling that he wasn't going with us. Dad would then react by berating him. Often, Mom would be so upset by it all that she would stay home and cook dinner. As I look back, it seems clear that the whole matter had little to do with church and a whole lot more to do with who was going to control whom.

Happy Childhood Memories

There were many happy times in my childhood. I spent countless hours playing with Deena and David, along with our only neighbors, Linda, little Charles, and Ann Culthberson, out on our shared mica-laden bank, making roads and villages for our toy cars. Deena and I would take our store-bought paper dolls and make whole families from the cardboard that came from our dad's laundered shirts. She and I played with those for hours in the hot afternoons.

My parents were not perfect at parenting; most important, though, they tried hard during our growing years to keep our lives stable and solid. At times, my dad lost his way in the day-to-day routine of family life, loading my working mother down with too many parenting responsibilities. My mother was caring but not affectionate toward us. She solved our sibling quarrels quickly and forcefully!

One way Mom showed her love for us was to cook very satisfying suppers for us. We were well fed on from scratch, home-cooked goodness; she never settled for less at home. Dad's routine was to come home much later, throw some food in one side of his mouth while telling mom about his day, then clear us kids out of the living room so he could play his organ in peace. Mom found it hard to break away from routine; however, Dad loved change, like few people I've ever seen do. He's the one who got us all out of the house to go camping, eventually making it all the way to the beach near Fort Lauderdale, Florida, multiple times during the sixties. We all were very appreciative to him for getting us out of the grind of our day-to-day lives.

Cherokee, North Carolina, and Achieving the American Dream

In the mid-sixties, my parents decided to move us to the Cherokee Indian Reservation located about forty miles west of Asheville. This, in time, proved to be a fortuitous move for my parents. We would always pass through Cherokee on our way to see my grandparents, but I don't recall that we ever shopped in the craft shops located there. Nevertheless, Dad believed that Mom could run one of those craft shops as well as anyone else could.

My mother was naturally gifted in left-brain thinking. (The left brain is where we solve math problems, keep up with details, remember names—in brief, it is the headquarters for all of our analytical thinking.) Our exodus out of Asheville proved to be a precursor to my parents' achieving the American Dream. Before that happened, though, we just simply got out of the house and got busy with summer jobs; we kids worked in Cherokee all of our teen years.

The store that my parents leased is completely gone today, but it sat across US 19 from the old Owl Motel and the big Old West town of Frontier Land just across the Oconoluftee River. Harrah's Casino eventually took over all the Frontier Land acreage and more.

At that time, the upper part of Cherokee was still very rural, with a few shops and old stores scattered among campgrounds and motels. For the first summer, we all lived in the back of the store, which had one large rectangular room with one small bedroom and a very small bathroom. During that summer, Dad and Mom found a used three-bedroom mobile home they put behind the store. It was the only house that my parents owned during all of my childhood.

David and I attended the old WPA-built Qualla elementary school that was located just off the reservation. We were both in the seventh grade then (David had been held back in the first grade). Mr. R. O. Wilson was our teacher, but he also taught the eighth-graders. There were about three rows of seventh-graders and about three rows of eighth-graders all in the same room. Mr. Wilson was the school's principal as well. The next year, we eighth-graders had doubled in population, so we took over the small auditorium and still had Mr. Wilson as both teacher and principal.

From there, we, along with all the other teenagers in Jackson County, attended Sylva-Webster High School in Sylva, where I now live. Back then though we lived about fifteen miles from our rural community, and it made for long, dreary bus rides during all of my four years there.

The Birth of Cherokee Sales Company Inc.

After a year of operating the small gift shop, Dad and Mom decided that she could run the old Tom Tom restaurant down on the strip while Deena and I ran the gift shop located about two miles away. Operating the Tom Tom with two shifts, seven days a week, lasted about three summers. Mom pretty much stayed at the restaurant seven days a week during the tourist season, and actually both of my parents basically lived there and visited home.

When they took over the restaurant, Dad still continued to sell for Hood Restaurant Supply Company but ran the cash register in his spare time. He moved one of his organs to the restaurant so he could play it in the evenings. Many times tourists would play beautiful melodies while waiting for their food.

The local souvenir shop owners became regulars at the Tom Tom, and it was through their friendships that Dad got the idea that he could wholesale souvenirs to the Cherokee gift shops. These friendships helped my parents find the vein of gold that was layered between the arduous labor and long hours it took to run two businesses.

At that time, there was no local supplier conveniently located near the reservation, nor was there much variety of souvenirs in any of the stores. All that was about to change, though, thanks to both of my parents' natural insight into the souvenir business and the forming of their very successful novelty wholesale company: Cherokee Sales Inc. The company has been located in the Whittier, North Carolina, area since the sixties and is quite a story in itself, evidence of how my parents naturally and often harmoniously formed and built a very stable business.

Cherokee Sales Company Incorporated

I don't know all the details of CSC Inc., but I do know the highlights of the story. When Dad found his first wholesale contacts, he didn't waste any time in buying a small pull-behind camper and loading it with samples. He started wholesaling in Cherokee but quickly went on to Gatlinburg and Pigeon Forge, spreading his territory out ever farther and farther. All of this took place starting in 1964.

Dad had two breakthroughs that changed his entire idea of selling. The first one came within a few years of being a sales rep for several companies. By then, he had figured out how to be a middleman, buying up large quantities of the latest quickest-selling fads as well as stockpiling the mainstay items such as feathered headdresses. This enabled him to provide a quick turnaround when supplying the shops.

By the time I graduated high school, Dad had gutted the living room area of an RV and turned it into a showroom. With the help of a carpenter, he made slanted, removable shelving from ceiling to floor. Each shelf fitted into a slot, and all were kept in place by vertical slats that were on hinges like doors. He covered each shelf with a large square of felt. Next, he attached souvenir samples onto the felt, and under each sample was a label with a name, cost per dozen, and the supplier name written in code.

He and Mom at one time traveled as far north as Lake Placid, New York, and as far south as the Gold Coast of Mississippi. They also sold as far west as parts of Kentucky.

Shortly after arriving back home, they started shipping the orders. This system worked for several years; my parents went through two RVs, and Dad currently owns a third one. The RV idea served both of my parents well because Mom hated restaurant food and loved a home feel to wherever she laid her head, and Dad, on the other hand, has always loved the footloose lifestyle that being on the road has to offer. Only after building the warehouse did they trim their traveling down.

Mom was an immense help to dad in several ways, one noticeable one was that they both were and are left-handed, but they were worlds apart on penmanship. Mom wrote the orders in a very neat left-hand slant, while my dad's scribble has always been nearly unreadable; only my mom was able to truly decipher it.

The next major breakthrough for them came when one of their souvenir jewelry suppliers in Miami took Dad on an overseas trip with him to both Japan and Hong Kong. He mentored and taught Dad the insider knowledge on how to go from being a sales rep to being an importer. This meant they would be able to increase their stock tremendously by having full shipping containers of souvenirs shipped directly to them from Asia.

My parents immediately borrowed larger amounts of money and went "whole-hog" into the souvenir import business. That gamble paid off well for them. My mother was always the more budget-minded of the two and kept up with the checkbook. I really believe they wouldn't have much today if she hadn't controlled the money as much as she was able to. That took a lot of standing up to Dad's arguing of wanting to spend, spend, spend!

To my dad's credit, he has been open-minded enough to be mentored by others, who were noticeably successful during his "learning times." Some of his ideas, though, wherever they came from, were not great ones. Mom had to endure his sexually suggestive choices in novelties for several years. Nevertheless, he did possess several books about selling. It's hard to believe, but he even had Dr. Norman Vincent Peale's book *The Power of Positive Thinking*.

They hired Gene to help Mom pack the orders and then he delivered them, while Dad spent his time selling. They rented vacant buildings as warehouses back then. In 1987, they built a nine-thousand-square-foot warehouse just off of the reservation and then hired my other brother, David, to help.

A few years later, they hired Carol as a salesperson, which worked out well, considering both of my parents had and have difficult but loving personalities. Over the years, she has contributed a lot of successful ideas to their souvenir line.

Dad really began to shine in his sales abilities when he and Mom owned their own company. Selling is the one thing he has always loved to do—though buying is a close second— and to this day he still does well at it. He learned the art of making a successful cold call in his early adolescence when he helped his dad sell ad space at the bottom of calendars to the stores in old Knoxville.

My mother always played a key role in the formation and ongoing operation of Cherokee Sales. She often chose jewelry and nontraditional gifts to add to their ever-expanding souvenir lines. Also, it was Mom who reigned in Dad's spending sprees and made it legal that Dad couldn't sign any checks by himself. Mom usually signed all the checks for both their personal and business bills. She told me that she paid off their spacious brick home and 4 acre tract within five years of building it!

Mom, Dad, Carol, Gene, and David formed a strong wholesale company. All but David, who didn't want to go, traveled to both the Atlanta Merchandise Mart and the Las Vegas gift shows buying wholesale lots for the company. For a few years, they (excluding David) also went once a year to China to a big wholesale show. Eventually, Dad began leaving Mom at home to keep watch over the warehouse for his own personal reasons.

In brief, over the course of four decades plus, my parents played a big role in changing the quantity, quality, and variety of souvenirs that are sold today in the Great Smokies. Also, another amazing fact about CSC Inc. is that with no more than three salespeople, one office person who assisted my mother, and three warehouse workers, my parents' company experienced many years of grossing over a million dollars in sales!

There were probably more setbacks than I'm aware of, but I know of two that had an effect upon the ongoing operation of the business. One happened in the winter of 2001, when the warehouse almost completely burned to the ground. Only the records and office equipment were salvageable. The small workforce moved to a large, well-built barn; added electricity; and quickly reordered most of its stock to fill pending orders. My family and I traveled up from our home in Sumter, South Carolina, to see the devastation for ourselves.

Shortly after the fire, though, Dad headed for China and stayed for several weeks, leaving my mom to deal with the bulk of the immediate insurance issues and reordering mire. Of course, since the invention of the Internet and e-mail, Dad has kept his finger on the pulse of CSC Inc. no matter where he is.

The other setback was my dad's random unfaithfulness to my mother. From time to time, a knife could cut the tension that hung in the air anywhere they were. Dad's poor moral choices had a way of affecting even the most innocent of bystanders at the warehouse. I know because I made the unwise decision of working for my parents on and off for a year or so after I had lost a social work position that I had held for a few months shortly after we had moved here.

When we still lived in South Carolina, visits to their home were not always pleasant experiences for me. I believe my parents subconsciously transferred the anger they had toward each other onto their children. Once, on a visit there with my family, I didn't complete all the morning chores that were expected of me. I thought I could get back to them later since all was done except doing my family's laundry. Gene had come over and wanted Jeff, me, and our girls to go hiking up in the Pisgah Forest with him, so I wadded up our dirty clothes and put them in a corner of our bedroom. As soon as I stepped back into their house, Mom stood about two inches from my face and threw a fit over that wad of filthy clothes that was left for her to finish. As much as I loved getting back to the mountains, it was hard to visit my parents for more than a few times a year.

The Original Hillbilly Calendar

I'm very proud to say that my parents invented the Original Hillbilly Calendar. It's a very popular, inexpensive calendar that has comical line drawings throughout of "Local Yokels." It's been sold throughout the Great Smokies tourist areas for more than thirty years!

It all came about on one sunny afternoon when my parents were sitting out on their patio after Sunday dinner. An idea came into my dad's mind when thinking about how mountain people always planned their days by the season that was coming up next; that way, they would always be ready for the next season whether it be planting, gardening, harvesting, or letting the ground and themselves rest.

Dad spent his childhood becoming streetwise growing up in the heart of old Knoxville. However, my mother grew up in the country and was very rooted in the southern Appalachian ways of life; Mom was a true highlander, being clannish about family, private about details, and certainly not the type to wear her feelings on her sleeves. It was always hard to tell if Mom was angry about something or just resting from the day and didn't want to be bothered.

As it was told to me, on that afternoon, Dad got to laughing about how we hillbillies do have our seasons for doing certain things, and the calendar idea just struck him: Hillbilly Calendars!

If you've never seen one, all the male hillbillies on each page look very much like hicks from the sticks with their patched coveralls, corncob pipes, and unkempt beards. Each hick is doing something comical. On several calendar days throughout each month, in print that looks more like scrawl, reminders are written such as when to take a bath, when to clean the gun for a shotgun wedding that's coming up, and when to cook and stir the mash for white lightning. (In my teen years, I tried a sip of white lightning. It was crystal clear like water but burnt all the way going down.)

After Dad sketched out his ideas on a legal pad, he then found a small book publisher in Arkansas and started mass-producing them. The rest is history.

My Angry, Loving, Caring Parents

When I think of my parents, I think of them as not being easily lovable. However, they have made up for their prickly nature by being dependable and steady, my mother more so than my dad. My mother was very routine and consistent. In my childhood, I believe it was her steadiness that was the glue that held the seven of us together. Just when it seemed we kids were about to declare sibling warfare, which would just about always include punching, kicking, and biting, she came with a belt. To my mother's credit, she whipped the biting habit right out of one of my brothers.

It seems to me that both of my parents were basically angry people who experienced periods of peace. Some anger in life is good. Justified anger makes us want to change things. Anger turned inward is depression, though, and anger turned outward is usually abuse.

Mom was a very high-stressed controller. Dad was angry but complacent about his role in our home. They both, I believe, transferred their unresolved anger onto us kids. This was a habit both of my parents fell into, partly because it kept them from having direct confrontation with each other over their marriage issues.

M. G. Bell, my dad, was one person Mom just wasn't going to control no matter how hard she tried. He seemed to always keep the upper hand by not falling in line with her timelines for supper or coming home after work within a reasonable time frame, among his other fallibilities.

Mom had a strong trait of obsessive compulsive disorder (OCD) within her personality. Things always had to be in a certain place, so we girls spent our time constantly picking up and cleaning. Even in her older years, visits to their home were stressful because my daughters' handprints would end up on every mirror in the house, a fact that was pointed out even though I always changed sheets, cleaned mirrors, and vacuumed before we left.

Even though we three girls and mom constantly cleaned, Dad didn't even bother to raise the toilet seat, consequently teaching my brothers not to respect us girls either. Carol and Deena started supper before Mom got home from work, and after supper I burned the nightly sack of garbage even when I was as young as eight years old. I don't know why one of my older brothers didn't have to do this task.

Home life often had the feel that it was stressful or about to get stressful. It just took one of my brothers' picking a fight for Mom or Dad to get the belt out. Then, both parties would get theirs!

My Mom Became a Victor

In honor of my mom, I want to say that I am the honest Christian woman I am today because of her. Her child-rearing tactics were rarely fair and often harsh; nevertheless, she tried hard and almost single-handedly kept us five walking the straight and narrow paths of our lives. Looking back, I'm sure that Mom was at times stretched to her breaking point.

During my childhood, Mom was diagnosed with ulcers and then overcame that diagnosis, no longer to be bothered by any major stomach problems. Later, she was diagnosed with rheumatoid arthritis—as I have been since—but she never took any medication for it!

Mom especially carried this victor attitude into their business. In order to slow or stop Dad's spending sprees, she eventually made it mandatory that two signatures be on any order forms or purchase payments. Much later in her life, she sought and gained sole ownership of all physical property previously held jointly by her and Dad. She also changed her will to include only us children. Mom resolved along her life's journey not to become a victim of Dad's mental-emotional abuse and manipulation and I'm very proud of her for doing that!

Being Raised to Live in Fear

I have some fairly painful memories of events that took place during my adolescence. I hesitate to include "war stories" but simply do so for the reader to understand, perhaps even relate to, why I spent one year in group counseling as well as two months in one-on-one therapy with a counselor.

The first severe memory I have somewhat reflects the relationship I had with my mother. While I was attending Qualla Elementary, my menstrual cycle began for the first time during a school day. Mom had avoided any talk of sex with me, so I didn't have too many clues as to why my body was changing. While getting ready for a bath later that day, I realized I had ruined my underwear. I clearly remember being on my knees crying and begging Mom not to whip me because I had ruined my panties. Right then and there, I got a one- or two-sentence instruction on the issue, and that summed up the only sex talk I ever got from her. There is an ever-unsolvable question I have whenever that memory floats into my mind: Mom had an extremely acute sense of smell, so without a doubt she smelled my cycle flow as soon as I got home from school yet said nothing to me. I will always wonder why Mom made it so difficult for me to enter into my adolescence. Nevertheless, I forgive my mother and have released any and all hard feelings I have ever had toward her.

The second strong memory I have of my teen years is of one of the last times Dad whipped me. I was fifteen years old, and we were living in the twelve-by-sixty mobile home then. It was about mid-afternoon on a Saturday, and I had gone down the long, narrow hallway to the bathroom from the living room to wash my hair. As I was coming out of the bathroom drying my hair with a towel, I passed David's bedroom. He and I had apparently exchanged words earlier, so he was ticked off and wanted to get even over something that I had said. As he was coming out of his bedroom, he pushed me into a hallway window, shattering it. Dad took his belt off and gave him a few strikes over his blue-jean-covered legs.

In the meantime, while juggling a wet towel still wrapped around my hair, I began picking up the shattered glass and throwing it in the kitchen garbage can that I had dragged down the hallway. Cleaning up our brothers' messes was expected of us girls. Once I had picked it all up, I vacuumed the entire hallway of green, patterned carpet. All the while, my dad was threatening me that my punishment was coming. As I entered the kitchen area, he grabbed my arm and began whipping my bare legs. I was crying and begging, "Please, stop, Daddy! I didn't start it!" Not until my knees hit the kitchen floor did "Daddy dearest" stop whipping me. My mother was standing to my left at the stove, cooking pinto beans and saying nothing. To this day, whenever I smell pinto beans, a complete image of that whole event, down to the furnishings, floats across my mind.

We had an orange semicircular couch then with lamp-style lights that were attached to the wall behind the long sofa section and with windows over the loveseat section. To my knowledge, no photos were ever taken of any of us during the time we lived inside that rectangular box, or at least I've never seen any.

The third abusive event took place during my late teens. Mom had finally broken free of the day-to-day tasks that come with keeping up with five children, something Dad had been pining for since he had begun selling. He frequently cornered me and said that he couldn't wait till I was old enough to move out and be on my own because he needed Mom to travel with him in his ever-expanding sales travels. Maybe that's why he didn't bother showing up at mine and David's high school graduation (same night, same place). I clearly remember him explaining to Mom that he just didn't think it was all that important to be there.

My parents had left on an extended business trip shortly after my brother and I graduated from high school, leaving us two by ourselves. Fortunately, he and I were both attending Southwestern Technical Institute (STI), but we went in separate directions after that. The problem was that there was only Mom's station wagon for us to share. It didn't take long for my brother's negative emotions toward me to come to the surface. He and I were out in the yard arguing about the car when he simply overpowered me. He threw me down on the ground and kicked me in my face several times before driving off in Mom's car.

I crawled into the trailer sobbing but managed to call my big sister Carol to ask her to please come and get me. I was afraid he was going to come back and finish beating me into the ground. I still remember my former brother-in-law, Wayne, scooping me off the couch and carrying me out to their yellow Mustang, saying, "Oh, my God, there was no need for this to happen."

I stayed with them for several weeks, sharing a room with their toddler, who we called Little Wayne. When I went back to school, a few fellow students told me that they would give me a ride to school if I was waiting out on the main highway at the time they went by where I was staying so that I wouldn't have to fight for the car.

When Mom and Dad returned home, Carol was instructed to bring me back home. I was to get in the car with my brother and continue attending school, acting like nothing had happened. And in their minds, maybe they thought nothing big had happened. They were removed from that violence by time, distance, and the fact that it hadn't happened to either of them. Also, they had had a big and very successful sales trip. It has always been sales that has fed my dad's (and consequently, my mother's) ego. Child rearing never seemed to have the kind of hold on them that sales did.

The way my parents handled this sad moment in my adolescence was to show very little respect for me. Fortunately, along with the bad, they were decent to me. I rarely cross paths with either of my brothers, so in case I don't say it at any other time, I'm saying here that I forgive both of them for the harsh way they have treated me throughout my life.

Aimlessness and Depression Are Related

After that painful last year at home, I moved down to Atlanta, Georgia. I did attend an art school but had no clear ambition to set and accomplish any goals. I really never knew how to make or reach a goal. My thoughts seemed detached from my actions. I was a very aimless person then.

I did learn about black-and-white development of both film and photos at the art school, which was located near Pershing Point, at about Sixteenth St. and Peachtree. Every morning, I walked by Margaret Mitchell's two-story brownstone where she wrote *Gone with the Wind*.

To sum it up, I didn't have a five- or a ten-year plan; I didn't even have a six-month plan at that point. All of my plans were no more than day-to-day plans. It took my sister Deena's moving to Atlanta a few years later to motivate and guide me into joining the Air Force.

I experienced at least one miracle during the years I lived in Atlanta and later in the area of Buckhead. I had moved to an apartment complex with two girls I had met at a boarding house where I had lived when I first moved there. Even though I wasn't much of a drinker, I got a little tipsy one evening at the pool and haphazardly went wading in. I remember suddenly realizing that it was too deep for me to touch bottom and yelling for someone to pull me out. I'm pretty much a rock in water. One of my two roommates, Denise, jumped in and pulled me out.

A Life-Saving Miracle Phone Call

At the end of that school year, I left Atlanta and nosedived into the very small and very southern Georgia town of Sandersville. I remember looking at signs that read "Whites Only"! I had stepped back in time in several ways. I worked for the only photographer in town at that time, Mr. Little. He and his wife ran a studio on Main Street. He was just another overbearing person in my life that I would add to my list of overbearing people that God seemed dead set on sending my way.

I did join a Baptist church there and attended regularly. I also quit smoking marijuana during that time. But the most unusual event that took place while I lived there was something that nearly cost me my life.

Since I didn't own a car, I had gotten a bicycle to get around town shortly after moving there. I moved into the second story of an old Victorian-style house and had my own outside entrance so no one knew when I came or went.

After leaving work one afternoon, I rode the short distance home, crossing a few roads along the way as usual. On one crossing, I had to dodge a car and ran up on a curb straight into some bushes! With that abrupt stop, my lower torso slammed into the metal bike frame. I didn't realize it then, but I was severely hurt. I knew I was bleeding. I made it up the stairs and into the antiquated bathroom where I tried desperately to wash off the blood, but it was unstoppable. Later, I learned that I had ripped my vulva and was bleeding internally, not externally like I kept thinking.

I'm telling the truth when I say that some two hundred miles away, God laid it on my sister Carol's heart to call me right then. I had been losing blood for some time. I answered the phone and out tumbled my desperate cry for her to send help.

Carol took control and called my employer to get someone over to my apartment quickly. When I woke up the next morning at the hospital, the first three people I saw were my parents and Carol. I was barely with it but was very glad to see them!

Life-Changing Events

In 1974, I moved back to Atlanta and worked at the Miesel Photo Processing Plant, which did color processing for most all the photography studios in Atlanta at that time. I got paid well, so I was able to move to an apartment on Lanier Boulevard, which is right off of North Highland Drive.

Lanier Boulevard was lined with well-built brick houses and tidy yards, quite a step up from the usual rundown places I had rented prior to then. Incidentally, North Highland runs into Morningside Drive, which is where *Driving Miss Daisy* was filmed.

My life was finally about to get on track. One important event was that my sister Deena and her first husband, Hal, had moved to Atlanta, so we saw each other frequently. I didn't much care for Hal, but he seemed to be part of the package that came with visiting my sister.

I was twenty-two and had become my own worst enemy. Nothing and almost no one I had been involved with had been good choices for me. I lost my job at Miesel within a few months of reconnecting with Deena and absolutely didn't know which way to go.

I owe the fact that I joined the Air Force to Deena. She believed in me and got me off the "couch of despair." I finally got focused on what I could do. Being four feet, ten inches tall didn't make it easy for me to join the military, but Deena kept encouraging me.

I was turned down by the Navy and didn't do well in an Army interview, but Deena wouldn't let up and said, "Aren't there more branches of service?" The Air Force had a big need for personnel as many of the Vietnam-era veterans were leaving, so they lowered their height requirements during the same time I was looking. I went for the test and performed well on reading very basic schematics. I enlisted in the early part of 1976 on delayed enlistment and began active duty in May of that year. Finally, I was able to get my life on a more stable footing from that time forward.

By the time I enlisted, Deena had broken free of Hal and was off to a great start on a new career and life as well. She was focusing on being a cosmetologist by attending night classes while working for the state of Georgia during the day. Deena has always been and continues to be both a great career and personal example for me.

The reasons I had gotten mired down in a sad lifestyle are not so much of a mystery to me now. But at that time, I couldn't have defined it, nor could anyone else who knew me. Knowing where I was going to lay my head down at night wasn't then and still isn't the cure for chronic melancholy or other types of depression.

Rekindling My Love for Christ

How I Overcame Chronic Dysthymic Depression isn't directly about spiritual issues, but there can never be complete healing in someone's life without addressing the spiritual side of healing. Some organizations call the spiritual side a higher power. I simply use the names God; Jesus Christ, his Son; and the Holy Spirit—the Holy Trinity.

One Sunday morning, I visited a nearby Baptist church and sat in a back pew. No one around me was dressed like I was, though. I looked every bit the long-haired hippie that I was, right down to my patched jeans and worn-out flip-flops. I was pretty much feeling out of place, and that was the general attitude of those I was sitting near, too. It just wasn't a good worship experience.

The next Sunday morning, I walked to where Lanier crosses North Highland and saw a church I had passed by often, but never took notice of. I felt led to go there and not long afterwards, Our Savior's Episcopal Church became my church. That was one of the friendliest churches I have ever attended. There were lots of young adults who went there, and all extended a very welcoming hand to me. Some were attending college, others worked; like me, many were figuring out what to do with their lives. For an introvert, I actually became sociable!

One Sunday after church, I invited a gal friend to my apartment for lunch. Andy (Andrea) was attending a nearby college, so over lunch I was telling her about my not knowing even enough math to pass an armed forces exam, hoping she had a solution to my dilemma. Andy didn't quite hear me, though, because God had allowed her to look into my very empty soul while I was rattling on about my problems. She bluntly told me to get rid of the drugs in my house and that it was time for me to really make a commitment to follow God. I dropped my fork at her pronouncement!

She had it right, though. It *was* time for me to start getting my spiritual life together. I remember quickly flushing my stash of weed down the toilet. Then Andy laid her hands on me and prayed over my new direction in life. Within a few Sundays, she graduated and moved back to Florida. I only saw her maybe five times altogether.

I became a member of the church and enjoyed the fellowship there. Within a few months, the rector organized several weekend Home Bible studies for a certain weekend with congregation meetings on Friday and Saturday evenings (something like a retreat idea). It was during this condensed event that I had a born-again experience.

Fall was in the air then. I remember leaves crunching under my feet as I went to one of the small-group meetings that were being held in nearby homes on Saturday. The entire church was excited, and there was a good turnout at all the different meetings. By the time I had walked back home Saturday night, I was exhausted. While resting, I remember praying a simple prayer to make sure I was saved. Right after that, I had a vision of Jesus coming into me!

I really grew in my Christianity during that year. Then I was off to the Air Force. Finally, Jesus was not only my Savior but also Lord of my life!

Moving to Spangdahlem Air Base, Germany

Being in the Air Force brought a lot of stability to my life. I finally quit going through the cycles of being unemployed and worrying about rent and my other bills. I was able to release myself from that stress and entered into a more consistently calm mind-set.

After my delayed enlistment was up, I went to Lackland Air Force Base in Texas for basic training. After eight weeks of that, I went to Chanute Air Force Base in Illinois for training to be a jet-engine mechanic. From there I went to Spangdahlem Air Base in Germany. I spent three years there and one year at Hill Air Force Base in Utah. By the time my first enlistment was up, I had met and married Jeff, and we had a baby on the way.

At "Spang" (what we all called Spangdahlem AFB), I worshipped at the base chapel, where I met a sprinkling of young Christian adults. There was such a small group of Christian singles at the chapel; I believe I was the only woman to walk the short distance from my dorm to the chapel on Sunday mornings for the first month or so.

The Christian organization the Navigators had a missionary couple living in a nearby village, and they had made some progress among the young men at the chapel. They were all kind to me, but I didn't feel included in their small-group Bible studies. Within a few weeks of attending the eleven o'clock services, I asked the head Protestant chaplain about starting a Sunday school class. Chaplain Lemuel Boyles was delighted at my request and stated that he'd like to teach it. This one idea began to bring a lot of young people together and not just on Sundays, either!

The Air Force was recruiting large numbers of young adults

during this time and opening up mechanical career fields to women as well, which is how I got in. By the time I asked about starting a Sunday morning Bible class, the trickle of young Christians was turning into a steady stream. Not only were single adults attending, but young married couples were coming too. We grew exponentially! Within a year of arriving there, I became very involved with the chapel and even started doing a children's church service during the eleven o'clock service along with another Christian.

All of us Christians had a great time, and since it was a small Air Force base, we all saw one another frequently throughout the week. During this time, I met Larry and Sue Porter. They started a Friday night praise service at the chapel. It was at that service that I first heard people praying in tongues and where I saw, for the first time in my life, someone fall flat on the floor. I was told that this experience is referred to as "being slain in the Spirit." It was different from anything I had ever seen or experienced, but I was okay with it all and attended the praise meeting frequently.

One of the many other outstanding Christians I met during this time is named Dan Robers. Dan was a part of the small Army detachment stationed there. He attended the chapel faithfully and had gotten to know a middle-aged couple who was attending there also with their three teen daughters. He admired the couple's spiritual maturity and asked them if he and a few friends could attend a Bible study at their base apartment. That request sounded good to Lionel "Lucky" and Marlene Lyons. Thus, the "Lyons' Den" was established.

"Lucky" and Marlene Lyons' Den

Lucky and Marlene Lyons launched a Sunday evening "Afterglow" after the seven o'clock service. It was a great time of fellowship that lasted for all the four years Lucky was stationed at nearby Bitburg Air Base. Never once did I hear they or their teen girls complain about traveling the fifteen miles to our chapel on Sunday nights to host the Afterglow.

Lucky and Marlene blended everything they did at the chapel into a seamless flow of extended chapel activities. They worked alongside Chaplain Boyles, and the three of them established Christian retreats at a hotel in Germany's Black Forest region for us. I still admire how unselfishly the Lyons gave of their selves while still being active, caring parents of their three daughters.

Lucky and Marlene built a strong fellowship among the young adults at Spangdahlem AFB during the four or so years they were there. With Jeff being a big fan of Facebook, we've found many of the "Spang" gang from the Lyons' Bible study group, and several of them have posted pictures. It's been fun finding out about the ones we remember and were close to.

Had depression left me? Not completely, because none of that great Christian fellowship and activity solved my main problem: undiagnosed chronic melancholy depression—depression so bad that I sometimes withdrew from fellowshipping with my friends. I missed several opportunities to be encouraged and lifted up in prayer.

When I would start to slip into that pattern of withdrawing from fellowship, God seemed to always put a fellow Christian in my path to guide me back into worshipping with other believers. I have several good memories of running into chapel friends and receiving encouragement from them. How did they know what to say just when I needed to hear it? Without a doubt, God placed them in my path to lift me up.

My husband, Jeff, and I met through the Sunday evening Afterglow service that the Lyons hosted. On Sunday mornings, he attended a church off base with his Christian roommate, "Flip" Flippen, but attended the on-base chapel in the evening. When Flip moved out, Jeff immediately got a new roommate, Duane Brownfield, who didn't attend church. Jeff witnessed to him and led him to the Lord.

Duane was very spiritually hungry and became active both in the chapel and in Lucky and Marlene's Bible studies. They became surrogate parents to Duane; as a matter of fact, they filled this parent role with many of the younger Christians. Both Lucky and Marlene liked being called Dad and Mom Lyons. It was Marlene who made my wedding dress, which I still keep in my closet.

> [A]nd let us consider how to stimulate one another to love and good deeds not forsaking our own assembling together, as is the habit of some, but encouraging one another; and all the more as you see the day drawing near. (Heb. 10:24–25 NAS)

God Created Marriage—We Add the Joy!

Three months after Jeffrey and I met, we were married at Spangdahlem Air Base Chapel. Both of us were new Christians when we met. Our dating was limited because neither of us had a car, but Jeff and I spent a lot of time walking through beautiful, deep woods. The base was located in western Germany near the ancient city of Trier. It is beautiful rolling hill country in that area.

Jeff and I got along well from the first. We were both in our mid-twenties, a little older than the rest of the young singles. It was our age, experiences, and perhaps even that we are both from the South that attracted us to each other. Affection blossomed into love, and we were married by Chaplain Boyles on August 4, 1978. By then, I really felt I knew him pretty well and am still in love with him now like I was then.

We both shared strong Christian beliefs, so we did not engage in sexual activity until after the wedding. My parents had visited for thirty days during our dating and were impressed with my southern beau. All seemed perfect or pretty close to it, and it was for several early years of our marriage.

The birth of our first child, Ruth, coincided with the end of my enlistment, and I was ready to be a stay-at-home mom and wife. She was pretty much the perfect first child from birth, never crying much beyond being hungry, and just wanted to be loved. Weighing in at a petite five pounds and six ounces, she was even the perfect size baby for me to deliver easily and naturally. When I switched her to solids, she willingly tried, at least once, every food I fed her. We were at Hill Air Force Base in Utah at that time and involved with Clearfield Baptist Church. Two years and one day after Ruth was born, our little blonde butterball, Rachel, was born, weighing in at seven pounds and eight ounces, and we were elated.

Around this time, Jeff had an overwhelming desire to leave the Air Force but wasn't sure what he would do next, so I stood in his way. Eventually, he saw my logic and stayed in a full twenty years. He actually enjoyed the military and received many outstanding performance reports over his enlistment. Once he retired, he was glad he had stayed in.

After Hill AFB, the four of us moved to Hahn AFB, which was located on beautiful rolling hills in West Germany. We moved to the quaint village of Rhaunen. During our three years there, we had Esther. She was the size of a small turkey, weighing eight pounds and two ounces at birth. Each daughter was nearly one pound heavier than the previous one. We were happy and felt that our quiver was full.

Next, we moved to Incirlik AFB in Turkey, where Jeff received the prestigious Military A.F. Achievement Medal. It is awarded to a military member who performs an action that goes beyond the call of duty. It all happened like this:

On a balmy Saturday morning while I was sipping my morning coffee, I noticed water seeping out from under the shared wall of our base housing. Our neighbors' apartment was flooding, and they had gone camping for the weekend. Yikes!

Jeff quickly got into their apartment and shut the water off. Then, he and nine-year-old Ruth started sweeping the water out and hanging wet stuffed toys and anything else that was soaked outside the windows. His commander got wind of his weekend heroics and nominated him for this prestigious award. I had the medal framed so he could proudly display it on a wall.

My Very Difficult In-Laws

Jeff's dad, Al, passed away while we were living in Turkey, and try as we might, it just proved to be too difficult to clear customs and arrive in time to attend his dad's funeral in Monroe, Georgia. We got there about three days too late for the funeral but still in time to see a beautiful array of flowers on my father-in-law's grave.

Jeff was the baby of three children born to Al (Albert) and Fran (Frances) Jordan. Their oldest child and only girl, Marilyn, had been born when Fran had just turned seventeen. She and Al had been married about a year by then. Their second child, a boy named Danny, was born when both Al and Fran had entered their thirties. Danny had an inoperable heart defect and wasn't expected to live very long, but he defied the odds and lived into his mid-teen years. He led a busy and full but all-too-brief life.

About four years after Danny was born, Jeffrey was born. By this time, Al was forty years old and starting to question where he was headed in his furniture sales career. He had a goal of one day operating his own business. He had done well in sales after trying a few other ideas in his early work life. He was taller than most men and heavyset. He had been blessed with a good, clear voice; a large, square, kindly face; and a matching disposition.

When Jeff entered his teen years, the family left Hapeville, a suburb of Atlanta, and moved to much smaller Monroe, where Al and Fran both had grown up. They purchased several acres there and built a block building that was partitioned off into a store and a small apartment. Later, they built a house near the store, and it's all still being used.

Their store was usually mostly empty except for a few chairs kept around an old wood-burning stove. Al made sales from a few sample books of carpet he kept on an old desk. Both he and Fran built their customer base on their good Christian character, having become active in their faith and in the Presbyterian Church in Hapeville shortly after their sons were born.

Neither Al nor Fran had finished school, but that didn't hold them back from succeeding at carpet sales and installation. Al had hit the carpet market at an amazingly good time, when people were starting to cover their hardwood floors with wall-to-wall carpet. Fortunately, he found good, dependable local help as well as Jeff, who learned the carpet business "from the floor up."

When Jeff graduated high school, he worked on and off for his dad laying carpet. Back then, when a customer wanted carpet, Al and Jeff would drive up to Dalton, Georgia, to get it and then lay it down in the customer's home the next day. It was, and still is, hard work; sometimes what was harder, though, was keeping Al from criticizing Jeff, who admired and loved his dad but had a difficult relationship with him.

Jeff's mom, Fran, was an angry, controlling person. Our visits to my in-laws' house were usually miserable experiences for me. By the time I had poured my first cup of coffee, Fran would have my day planned. I simply chose not to participate in as much as it was possible to do so. For me, those were depressive visits.

By the time I knew them, Al and Fran were financially secure, having done well during their carpet store heydays. Neither of them ever owned a new vehicle, and they built their house as they had money to build it, so there was no mortgage to pay off. They both lived a very frugal and seemingly contented life.

Unfortunately, though, Fran had a strong tendency to live in the past. She always seemed to be upset about having to leave her tidy little house in Hapeville so Al could realize his dream of having his own carpet store. They had two entirely different levels of ambition, and Fran was a clingy, dominating controller.

Al often earned recognition as Salesman of the Week at furniture stores around Hapeville and had a strong natural intuition for how successful carpet stores needed to operate. Nevertheless, Fran often held Al back from achieving his goal of his own store because moving back to Monroe was not what she wanted at all. Eventually, by the time Al turned fifty-five, he had pried Fran out of their house and moved them to Monroe. He quickly got his carpet store up and running.

In the early nineties, after she had become a widow, Fran expressed that she was somewhat glad Al had moved them to Monroe. After having been "dragged" to Hapeville somewhat against my will, even I could see that she was actually safer and better off having moved, even though she still occasionally complained about it all. Her daughter, Marilyn, and Marilyn's husband, George, had built a mother-in-law suite on their house and moved her there. Their three adult children (Fran's grandchildren) lived close by and all checked on her and visited often. Even after I quit going, I made sure Jeff traveled there every few months for a weekend visit during the thirteen years we lived in Sumter, South Carolina.

Forgiving Difficult Relatives!

While our girls were still quite young, I began feeling high levels of stress. One thing I did to address it was stop visiting Fran. It was the only way I could stop her verbal attacks on me. I was never rude or snide to her and always treated her with the respect due an older person, as I had been taught to do.

I believe my mother-in-law subconsciously shifted into an alter-personality when tension was in the air. Perhaps, also, I represented the fact that life had moved on and she couldn't hold on to a particular time frame except through her memories. As I've stated earlier, Fran was overtly clingy, which "brushed up against me" as I was not raised by clingy people.

These revelations came to me through a year's worth of counseling I received a few decades later. Through therapy, I've been able to understand personality disorders and therefore forgive her more completely than I had been able to before.

> Beloved, let us love one another, for love is from God; and everyone who loves is born of God and knows God. (1 John 4:7 NAS)

What Do We Do with Our Anger?

Arguing is a type of low-grade fighting that families do. A person who habitually argues is usually an angry person. Stasha, a licensed therapist whom I've seen, is the originator of those two thoughts; I heartily agree, though! This has been my personal experience, and I don't think my family or my extended family is that much different from most any others out there, regardless of where we live.

To my husband's credit, he has become more willing to listen and less of an arguer through the years, thank goodness! But for years, I had to remind him that I was allowed to have my own opinion in my own home—and here in America as well. He had subconsciously developed an argumentative style of communication early in his youth, and I had equally strongly developed a "defend-and-explain" style of communication. Our everyday communication would often bring on a stress headache for me!

I had less confrontation the few times I went before a judicial hearing and represented my church, Shaw Heights Baptist, in opposing a new bar right outside the housing gate at Shaw Air Force Base in South Carolina than I had with Jeff. He would agree with that now that he's experienced healing from his own unresolved issues.

I have read several good books on how to manage anger and to get beyond being depressed. One book I recommend is *Battlefield of the Mind* by Joyce Myer. I've read so many good books on healing from depression that it's hard to remember what I've learned from each book.

The obvious first thing anyone needs to do, though, before reading any book, is to admit that he or she is an angry or depressed person. Who knows where or how anger or depression starts in a person's soul or psyche.

Another book that Jeff and I read together is *Angry Men and the Women Who Love Them* by Dr. Paul Hegstrom, PhD. Dr. Hegstrom writes from firsthand experience but also from his professional counseling experience. And Steve Arterburn's radio show on Sirius has helped Jeff and thousands of others to receive healing from being angry.

Trademarks We're Known By

My trademarks have been that I spent too much time trying to fix and repair Jeff's flaws (or perceived flaws), which did create some unnecessary marital tension between us; he became more stubborn the more I sought to change any of his negative attitudes and to help increase his vision of himself. Eventually, and fortunately he saw my logic on most issues and shifted more towards the agreeable middle on what was important. I needed to define, in my thoughts, what truly was important and to let go of what truly wasn't. I felt that I could see Jeff's potential maybe better than he could; and that thinking process helped me to eventually "see" my own potential, which led me back to attending college.

We must've had subconsciously achieved much of agreeing "in the middle" because, for the most part, we both are very happy with our lives together. I have always optimistically believed that our issues would all get worked out in the end, and it usually has happened just that way.

In my childhood, I learned how to compartmentalize my troubles and then spend my time trying to please the discontented person with my exhaustive efforts. I subconsciously taught myself to fix and own any and every problem. Doing this kept me from confronting my own emotional baggage and to withdraw into my short-sighted, depressive shell. At that time, I didn't know how to behave any other way.

One of Jeff's trademarks is that he is a good and moral Christian man. To his very core, he has always sought to please God. Our shared Christian faith, our love for each other, and our love for our children, and now grandchildren have kept us moving in the same direction for well over three decades now.

Both of Our Attitudes Needed Changing

I believe we live years of our lives guided by our day-to-day attitudes, be they good or bad.

I used to think when my girls were much younger, "Oh, today is going to be different than all the others. The coffee is perfect, the sun is out, the kids are sleeping late; this is the perfect day for me to get a fresh start on my problem solving." The problem was that that day ended up meshing into all the others, with little or no change taking place. I kept carrying around the same old baggage I had struggled with and never confronted my real issues, while life itself placed ever more responsibilities on me.

Sooner is always better than later for checking our attitudes and being honest about the big picture that shows our own personal lives. My life, like yours, is not an island, I innermesh with my family every day in some way. Do all you can to avoid self-centered behavior, criticizing remarks, and/or blaming others. Each of these negative attitudes is always harmful to all they touch. Be aware that what you say and how you say it affects others. Ask yourself, "Is what I'm about to say the TRUTH? Am I helping or hindering my relationships or friendships?"

Benefits of Successful Counseling

When we were younger, neither Jeff nor I were well equipped to heal our own deep wounds. The difference today is that both he and I have been to counseling, and we talk about what we've learned through that counseling more openly now. We both realize that it took counseling for us to release our anger and depression in positive ways. Without it, we would have kept being our own or each other's worst enemies without meaning to be. Counseling has truly enriched our lives and set us free.

Not many of us are truly able to understand what lies beneath the surface of our loved ones, or even our own selves, for that matter. Sometimes it's good for us to step back, see the bigger picture, and think, *I wonder what provoked my loved one (or me) to say that or be hurtful?* We suppress our bad memories for decades of our lives yet wonder why we're not reaching our goal of happiness in our marriages, family, work, or our other endeavors. It seems clear to me that we usually react to the dominant personality that's within our circles, especially so when we are young and vulnerable.

The truth can be found through some good counseling. Living in truth will always bring peace! One thing I do that keeps me focused on seeking truth is journaling. I journal my prayer concerns and dreams, mostly. I've found that works for me in releasing my stress and anxieties, plus it helps me to focus on the real issues. As a bonus, I can look back over my prayer requests and record how God has answered many of them.

When our girls were teens, a school counselor called me to see if we would take one of them to counseling. I agreed, and those sessions changed both of our paradigms of counseling for the better.

First Grade 1958

P.A. Bell
Lackland AFB

Basic Training Graduation

Honorable Discharge

from the Armed Forces of the United States of America

This is to certify that

PATRICIA A. JORDAN, SGT, FR, REGULAR AIR FORCE

was Honorably Discharged from the

United States Air Force

on the 19th day of May 1980. *This certificate is awarded as a testimonial of Honest and Faithful Service*

James M. Jones Jr.
JAMES M. JONES, JR., Major, USAF
Chief of Military Personnel

DD FORM 256 AF
1 NOV 51

THIS IS AN IMPORTANT RECORD – SAFEGUARD IT!

Beglaubigte Abschrift -Auszug*)- aus dem Familienbuch

J o r d a n
Ehename (ggf. Familienname des Mannes)
B e l l
Geburtsname des anderen Ehegatten (ggf. Familienname der Frau)

1. Ehemann:

Familienname	Jordan -/-
v. d. Eheschl. Vornamen	Jeffrey Alan -/-
Beruf	Senior Airman -/-
Geburtstag	9. März 1952 -/-
Geburtsort	Fulton, Staat Georgia, USA -/-
Standesamt, Nr.	Einwohnermeldeamt von Atlanta Nr. 2894 60 2885, protestantisch -/-
Grundlage der Eintragung	-/-

2. Ehefrau:

Familienname	Bell -/-
Vornamen	Patricia Adrian -/-
Beruf	Airman first class -/-
Geburtstag	5. Mai 1952 -/-
Geburtsort	Cherokee, North Carolina, USA -/-
Standesamt, Nr.	Einwohnermeldeamt von Cherokee Nr. 20-57, protestantisch -/-
Grundlage der Eintragung	-/-

3. Eheschließung Eheschließungstag, -ort 24. Juli 1978 in Speicher -/-
Grundlage der Eintragung Heir.Eintr. Nr. 26/1978, St.Amt Speicher -/-
von 1 und 2

4. Eltern des Ehemanns:

Vater:
Familienname: Jordan -/-
Vornamen: Albert Walter -/-
Wohnort oder letzter Wohnort: Monroe, Staat Georgia, USA -/-
Grundlage der Eintragung: Geb.Urk. zu 1 -/-

Mutter:
Familienname: Jordan geb. Fambrough -/-
Vornamen: Frances -/-
Wohnort oder letzter Wohnort: Monroe, Staat Georgia, USA -/-
Grundlage der Eintragung: Geb.Urk. zu 1 -/-

5. Eltern der Ehefrau:

Vater:
Familienname: Bell -/-
Vornamen: Myron G. -/-
Wohnort oder letzter Wohnort: Cherokee, North Carolina, USA -/-

Mutter:
Familienname: Bell geb. Lloyd -/-
Vornamen: Myrtle Jean -/-
Wohnort oder letzter Wohnort: Cherokee, North Carolina, USA -/-
Grundlage der Eintragung: Geb.Urk. zu 2 -/-

8. Angelegt: -/-

Speicher, den 24. Juli 1978

(Siegel)

Der Standesbeamte
gez. Meyer

*) Nichtzutreffendes streichen

Marriage Certificate

Wedding 1978. Front row: Me, Jeff, Wanda (Plummer) Neilson, Duane Brownfield, Back row: Joe ?, Joko Tasich, Chaplain Boyles, Marlene Lyons, and Penny Phillips

First Family Photo 1985

Suffering from Deep Depression 1991

After family counseling 1998

Coker College

hereby confers upon

Patricia Bell Jordan

the degree of

Bachelor of Arts

with all the rights, privileges and honors appertaining thereto. In Testimony Whereof, the Seal of the College and the signatures as authorized by the Board of Trustees are hereunto affixed. Given at Hartsville, South Carolina, this thirteenth day of May, two thousand.

Chairman, Board of Trustees

President of the College

Graduation from Coker College 2000

My parents mid 90s

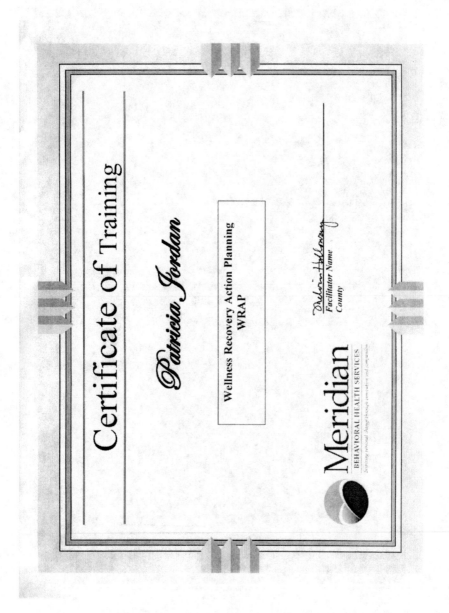

WRAP Counseling certificate

Front row l-r Gene, Carol, me, Deena, and David. Back row is Uncle Buddy and Aunt Dorothy (Bell) Crisp, Mom, Dad, and Grandma Chenault about 1960. Many of my friends notice the hard edge Mom had began to show.

My mom, June Lloyd. Photo taken at her graduation from Knoxville Business College in 1946, right before she had married dad.

Dad and Mom about 1946 in front of old Knoxville Bridge

Jeff, Rachel, and Me holding our first grandchild Mia in SC 2002.

Me with Creme Puff, Esther, Rachel, and my brother Gene in front of Johnson family church my maternal granny attended in her childhood.

Me, Esther, Mom, and Ruth about 2005

My maternal grandparents Dewey and Myrtle (Johnson) Lloyd about 1920

My paternal grandmother Etta (Jones-Bell) Chenault with Dad about 1945

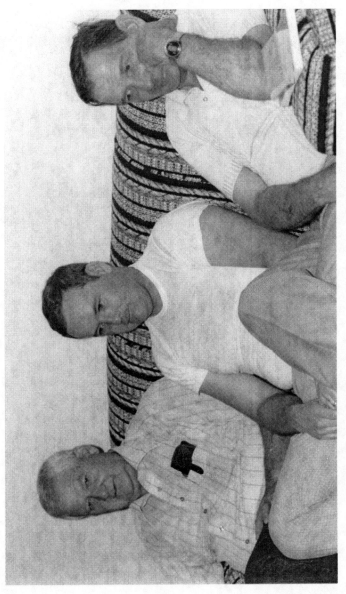

l-r Jeff's dad Al, Jeff, and my Dad when Ruth was born, 1980. (They all visited us in Utah but I couldn't find any photos of Jeff's mom Fran.)

Jeff, Me, and Skeeter at Fontana Dam

Taking Ownership of My Issues

During most of my children's younger years, I was able to function around the edges of a fairly normal life, but I lacked joy and a feeling of being connected. Often I didn't even go to church, and if I did, I had it down to about fifty minutes of worship time for the week. Otherwise, I stayed in my house.

My depression was hard for many to notice because I filled my days with the usual activities. I cooked hot meals, never stayed in bed all day (a sign of deep depression), kept a tidy house, kept spending to a minimum, and even walked my dogs. If simply doing good things and being a good person solved depression, then I would have solved mine all on my own.

I couldn't admit even to myself that I suffered from depression. I also avoided the marriage communication problems that Jeff and I had. By being non-confrontational, I enabled Jeff to avoid facing his anger. I did my best to make him happy, never understanding the real source of his discontent, which was unresolved anger about issues from his past and a lack of closure over his brother dying in his childhood. Jeff can still recall that few people visited them immediately after Danny's death, even their minister stayed completely away!

I gradually came to realize that our negative emotions are internal decisions rarely corrected without self honesty and a great amount of self- effort. I might have found the answer I deeply needed by reaching out to our pastor, Rev. Cheek, and letting him know of my two-fold dilemma of depression and living with a husband who was quick to criticize. I had plenty of opportunities for even a quick talk, and our pastor knew us both, as we were both involved in our church along with our teenage daughters.

Jeff and I did see a counselor, and it was a good start,

but the therapist barely touched on my blue moods or his unexplained bouts of anger. She did help us to develop effective communication habits, though.

Many years later on, Jeff and I both have gone, at different times, to Meridian Behavioral Health to attend group and individual counseling. Their programs work best for each of us because they offer many different kinds throughout the week and each one is ongoing. A peer counselor will help find the right classes for each person who attends and then becomes a life coach for each student at Meridian.

To Jeff's credit, he has also sought out Christian counselor Elizabeth Dewees, LCPC, for individual counseling. She operates her own Christ-Centered Counseling Center locally and can be found on Facebook.

My Emotional Healing

I didn't believe in myself when I became an adult. I didn't know how to get above basic survival living. I believed I could have just enough mental and emotional peace to get by. I had little idea how to thrive and flourish.

I often felt disconnected in my parenting. Many times when my family and I went to Myrtle Beach, I walked our dog around the crepe myrtle trees while Jeff was down at the beach splashing in the surf with our girls and having fun.

I spent two years sitting in my new brick home in Sumter thinking that I would just as soon kill myself as not. I was forty-two when that mental battle started. Just prior to this time, I had my uterus removed because of cancer, which affected my moods. Nevertheless, God pulled me through that deep depression by constantly reminding me of how much my family loves me and how much I love them.

It was an intense time for me that's still hard to talk about. During those two years, Jeff and I attended several sessions of marriage counseling, which helped both of us greatly. And as I mentioned, I stopped visiting my mother-in-law, who lived four hours away. I simply couldn't take her criticisms of me.

Toward the end of those two years, I started my college career. Deep Dysthymic depression tends to last up to two years. I likely was coming out of it then, considering all I got accomplished shortly after those intense two years.

How I Learned to Avoid, Deny, and Enable

I believe where there is a tendency for one person to become overly responsible, then there is a natural reaction on another's part to become less responsible. This is the best definition I can think of to describe what being an enabler is. In my childhood, I learned to take ownership of others' irresponsible actions as if I could fix their habits or even their personalities.

Subconsciously, I learned to compartmentalize my stress and anxieties so as to avoid conflict and also to avoid the acknowledgement that I even had an emotional problem. I learned this by being under my mother's dominating, controlling influence. Through the years, she also became an enabler of my dad's indulgences and my brothers' bad attitudes. Also, both of my parents transferred a lot of their anger and frustrations onto us kids.

The mental maneuvering of denying and avoiding conflict keeps our problems from going away, making sure they will never be successfully resolved. Mine just kept piling up, becoming a heavier burden for me to carry every day of my life.

This "deny-avoid-enable" problem-solving strategy nearly ruined my mental health in my forties. Living with a husband whose discontent could rise like an ocean wave, plus my own state of disconnected sadness, almost broke me. Notice that I say *almost*.

The Importance of Acceptance and Validation

We all need both acceptance and validation from others. No one is an island. What we don't need is someone to constantly criticize us. We all need others in our lives who love us just the way we are. Everyone needs to be built up by receiving compliments that speak truth, encouragement, and contentment. It is so very important that we validate one another. Christians are specifically called to "stimulate one another to love and good deeds" (Heb. 10:24).

All through my childhood, I seemed to be just a few steps away from having my parents tell me that I was okay and that I was loved. Instead, each chose to give out constant criticism of not only me but all of their five children. It just wasn't in my parents to build their children up. Dad has always seen his interpersonal relationships as though they are on a win-or-lose basis. He had to criticize one of us in order to make himself feel like a winner. The effect that had on Mom was that the longer she stayed married to him, the angrier she became—not so much at him but usually at her children, warehouse workers, grandchildren, and so on.

Jeff could barely get over his own childhood wounds enough to understand and be who I needed him to be. Yes, he could have been more understanding, and I wish he had been. Still, what I needed was a deep healing, which happened when I went to therapy. When Jeff became aware of my childhood wounds, his attitude began improving. Eventually, while he was recovering from his atrial fibrillation, he went to Meridian often and received his own healing that he hadn't even been looking for.

When I attended classes at Meridian, I began breaking

bad communication habits I had practiced throughout my life. I achieved this through attending group and individual counseling, increasing my reading of self-help books, and journaling. Through all this effort, plus prayer and getting back into regular church attendance, I've broken many of those self-defeating habits of communication that I subconsciously practiced. Recognizing and admitting what my deepest wounds were helped me to purposefully seek out healing in those areas with positive and healing messages.

Shifting My Paradigm from Victim to Victor

I have received counseling for depression at various times in my adult life. The earliest counseling sessions happened when a middle-school counselor called me one day with concerns about one of my daughters. I heard the sincerity in her voice, and it was the right moment for me to really hear the depth of what she was truly saying to me.

Within a short while, I made an appointment for Jeff, myself, and our three daughters at a family counselor's office. Jeff's insurance covered ten sessions, and I can't say I willingly went to all of them, probably because I was going through a depressive cycle. Nevertheless, Dr. Gail quickly weeded out our well-behaved polite teen daughters as the source of any major problem and focused right in on Jeff and me. It does seem odd that she didn't notice I was depressed.

One technique she used for improving our communication with each other was for each of us to talk to an empty chair, envisioning one of our parents in the chair. This was a chance to look at the past and was a guided opportunity for us to direct whatever anger or other feelings we had toward the appropriate parent. This didn't have much effect on me at that time, though years later that same technique proved to be very successful with me. But for Jeff, this particular session proved to be a very good thing. I saw my husband openly weep while he told his deceased dad good-bye and forgave his mom for burying his dad before we could get home from overseas. This happened some five years after Jeff's dad had been buried. That session was perhaps the best one!

During those ten sessions, we both learned some good techniques for positive communication. I didn't know how to release my negative emotions, though, so I stayed tightly wound and defensive most of the time. That's the only way I had ever known to behave. We solved some other issues that we had both kept stumbling over. I wanted to go to college and acquire a degree in social work, and it was Dr. Gail who expressed to Jeff—and encouraged me as well—just how important it was for me to have another life outside of being a homemaker. She also encouraged Jeff to start using his GI Bill by taking college classes himself on base. Jeff did that exact thing and two years later graduated with an Associate's Degree in Criminology. Her insight was what both of us needed.

Solving My ADD

Attention deficit disorder (ADD) has been proven to be an actual learning issue. I hate to hear people argue over whether it exists or not. It does, and like one of my brothers, I've suffered from it, but not as badly. It's very clear to me that it is genetically passed down through the generations. My dad, one brother, a nephew, my daughter Esther, and I have all struggled with this unseen issue that makes learning difficult.

As for me, I've never been diagnosed with ADD. Understanding what it is and appropriately treating it came well after my brother and I finished school. I came into the understanding of what it is only by researching it for my daughter's sake. I wanted to be an informed parent, especially since treating it involved giving her Ritalin. In learning about it, I saw myself.

I can only describe my personal experience with this learning issue. I've never been a detailed thinker. My mind glazes over when I'm bogged down with details. I was born a big-picture, right-brain thinker, like my dad. And just like him, I've never kept my focus on anything for long, often forgetting what I was supposed to do or get. I've also often spoken impulsively, which I consciously make an effort not to do. All of these are trademarks of ADD.

Perhaps I've subconsciously compensated for having ADD by drinking black coffee ever since I was teenager. I find coffee a powerful mental stimulant and have, for decades, drunk copious amounts of it throughout my day. Also, today I take an herbal mix that includes gingko for mental sharpness. I discovered how helpful gingko is when I took night classes to complete my degree.

In my childhood, I was simply considered a slow learner by

my teachers as well as my parents. That may have been one reason that I didn't try to achieve anything above mediocrity in my classwork; I subconsciously wore that wrongful label. One of my early teachers wanted to hold me back, but to my mother's credit, she argued against it and won.

By the time we moved to Cherokee, when I was twelve, it was clear that I didn't do well with understanding details. The first couple of summers, I helped Mom in the souvenir shop while my siblings found summer jobs elsewhere. Mom tried to teach me how to count out change from a sale, which is one of the few memories I have of my mother touching me: she laid money in my hand for me to practice with.

Over and over, we played this tedious game so I could learn how to count change. It was a near disaster for me. Naturally, I made many mistakes, and just as naturally, my mother constantly told me how mentally slow she thought I was. I do remember eventually learning it, though.

It would be decades later that I would tell my parents how having undiagnosed ADD negatively affected me. My self-esteem was nearly crushed by constantly being told by both of my parents that I was "never going to measure up" to their (sad) standards. Of course, today, I look back with forgiveness. No one knew what to call those vague, unseen learning disabilities back then.

Attention Deficit Disorder in My Family

A few years after I graduated the eighth grade, my former teacher, Mr. Wilson, helped my oldest brother, Gene, get into the newly formed community college in Sylva. In the sixties, no one knew what to call the learning issue now known as ADD or ADHD. Gene got a dose of Dad's ADD, and, like Dad, he turned it into a positive rather than a negative.

When they were in high school, Carol tutored Gene just to keep Dad (the high school drop-out) from yelling at him to "just get the blank-blank homework done!" But even with Carol's help, it was hard for Gene to keep his focus in class.

After graduating, Gene wanted to attend the TV repair class that STI was offering. His grades hadn't pleased the admission board, but Mr. Wilson went to bat for Gene and got him enrolled in the program. I'm proud to say that my brother did so well in that one-year class that the school helped him get into the more advanced training at Greenville Tech down in South Carolina. He never missed being on the honor roll that year, to the best of my memory. We ADD people can do pretty well once we find our true interest, whether it's in our workplaces or pursuing our personal interests.

My Daughter Was Diagnosed with ADD

In the early nineties, my daughter Esther started school at Oakland Elementary in Sumter. It seemed that she had a learning problem similar to what my brother and I have. Jeff and I didn't worry about her lack of focus in kindergarten, but in her first-grade year, we realized that she had a very real learning roadblock. Her teacher was becoming very frustrated with her inability to finish a simple sheet of coloring. Neither Jeff nor I knew how to help her, either.

It was then that I began seeking answers. A teacher in our church suggested that I take "Es" to a pediatrician, which I did. The military doctor was a lieutenant colonel who had been a pediatrician for a few decades. I felt I could trust his judgment and was glad I did. He looked over her classwork, which was mostly unfinished if started at all, and stated that she likely had ADD. At the time, Ritalin was the common answer, and he prescribed a very low dose for her, which I made sure she took every morning.

Prior to this, Es had barely connected with her teacher or even her young classmates; she was quiet and mostly looked out the window or down at her desk. Once she started taking Ritalin, we saw a much more connected child throughout the day.

After she had been on it for several weeks, her music teacher, Ms. Grabil, stopped me in the hallway and somewhat jokingly told me about the new little blonde singer she had just discovered among her first-graders, which of course was Esther! In addition to the other affirmations from school staff, I was greatly pleased to hear her tell me that I (and eventually her dad, too) had made a right choice for her.

Placing her on Ritalin was not an easy decision to make. Since this was before the Internet was widely available, our information on Ritalin was limited. Jeff was not as quick to seek out an answer as I was; I think he hoped she would naturally grow out of it. I didn't think she would, though, based on my own childhood experiences and seeing how much stress undiagnosed ADD added to both my life and my family life while growing up.

Actually, Jeff and I both were a little right about the issue. Eventually, many kids do grow out of ADD that affects their everyday lives. Perhaps puberty has something to do with the "growing out of it" aspect. However, what I saw was a struggling first-grader who needed our immediate help.

Eventually, Es did stop taking Ritalin and was able to graduate from Crestwood High School as a result of her own, unadulterated cognitive efforts. Coming off Ritalin in her teen years was her own decision. School studies took a great deal of concentration on her part after that, and she was still active in the marching band and holding down a part-time job as well. She made a good decision then, as I had earlier. None of us three have any regrets about our decisions.

The Importance of Positive Healing Messages

After I graduated from Coker College, I worked with troubled youth at a treatment center in South Carolina. While there, I read a series of paperbacks that the girls were reading; they were written by Dave Peltzer and were about his abusive childhood. The first book is called *A Child Called "It."* After reading it, I knew that I would not have made it in Dave's childhood home. I would have been crushed by the kind of depraved family life that Dave experienced as a child. Yet he went on to have a successful career. Dave's autobiography is written for the adolescent and is very moving—well worth the read. During his teen years, he had a few positive foster-parent influences in the mix that helped him in making good choices for his life.

I'm a big reader of biographies. I'm always on the lookout in particular for stories of a life redeemed, of tough circumstances turned around for a positive outcome. I recently read *Embrace the Struggle* written by Christian motivational speaker Zig Ziglar. He fell down a flight of steps a few years before writing it and needed a brain shunt. Believe it or not, Ziglar turned that harsh experience around to a positive, as he describes in his book. He has written several books that can be found cheaply enough in used-book stores or on websites.

I can't possibly mention all the spiritually uplifting books I've read or what all I've gained from them, but the important message here is that we need to feed our minds with believable, positive messages. I choose Christian teachings because I want to stand on solid ground whenever I start searching for solid answers.

In my youth, I read non-Christian writers only to have each

one not satisfy my searching thoughts and questions. None healed my wounds. I'm not satisfied with seemingly digressive conversations on existentialism or other never-ending dialogues on philosophical ideologies.

I'm only here on planet Earth for a limited time, like everyone else, and I don't want to waste my time on weighty discussions about subjects that are not clear-cut. I prefer to read about how Christians triumph over human tragedies that truly seem inevitable, how they "let go and let God" take over. That is something that I as well as others can and absolutely will be uplifted by.

Most important for me is daily Bible reading, as it has been throughout my adult life. Many times, God's Word has carried me over troubled waters with an exact verse that I absolutely needed for that day. I've read and searched the Bible through and embraced its truths time and again. God's Word continues to stand the test of time and always renews and refreshes my thirsty soul, as it will yours too.

This Scripture makes it clear just what Jesus has done for us and what God will do for us as believers.

> But He *was* wounded for our transgressions,
> *He was* bruised for our iniquities;
> The chastisement for our peace *was* upon Him,
> And by His stripes we are healed.
> (Isa. 53:5 New King James Version)

Moving to Western North Carolina

After the girls grew up and moved away, I didn't want to stay in South Carolina any longer. I felt a deep longing in my soul to return to the Great Smoky Mountains, where I had been raised. So Jeff and I sold our house and moved to Sylva, North Carolina. I felt better about everything after we moved back to the place I've always called home.

About a year later, Jeff's then current job working a bread route started not to look very promising. I suggested that he try becoming an eighteen-wheel-truck driver. Jeff has always been a good driver and drove a lot of different vehicles in the Air Force. We found a good school over in Asheville and he still had some GI Bill education money left. All that worked out exceedingly well. Actually, better than we had planned!

Before he could get his commercial driver's license (CDL), he had to pass a health screening. This is where he was told that his blood pressure was high—really high. I'll always say that trucking literally saved Jeff's life. Undoubtedly, he was headed for early and serious health problems related to unchecked high blood pressure.

When Jeff got his blood pressure under control and continued driving, he had time to think out on the road and took a serious inventory of his life. It would really be better for him to tell his complete story of being healed of his angry nature, but that would be a book in itself.

It did take a few years for everything to gel for him. First, he had to get used to pulling up to forty-four thousand pounds of weight around, as well as being on the road for several weeks at a time. Eventually, though, he had to face himself since there were very few distractions in his day. After a few years, we got him Sirius radio, which helps with the loneliness of being on the road.

Once he had six months' experience under his belt, he switched to Averitt Express, which makes a good effort to get their drivers home every weekend. This has made it possible for him to get involved with our church's praise band on Sundays, and he's been with Averitt for several years now.

Deep Sleep Test

After Jeff experienced atrial fibrillation (similar to a mild heart attack), he went in for a sleep test. The results were not good! They revealed that he barely ever got any real amount of deep sleep. In fact, his heart had actually stopped a few times while he was sleeping. His snoring has always been atrocious, and that coupled with being overweight meant that he likely had sleep apnea. The test confirmed it. Today, he sleeps very restfully with a CPAP machine and has a much calmer temperament.

Closure

While he was convalescing, he went to therapy with me several times, and we were able to help some old wounds heal. I felt so much better from these joint counseling sessions that I felt talked out, and it was then that I became determined to get my story out there. It's 12:43 a.m. right now, and I've probably written five new pages since I sat down, as well as proofread some previous ones. I write strictly from my memory, or as the Spirit leads, except for the Bible quotes I've included.

What Are the Signs of Depression?

Detachment—that one word sums up so much about how I have felt many times in my life. My children all too frequently saying during their teen years, "Mom, I've asked you twice already! Are you even listening to me?" still rings in my memory. Too often, I gave them blank stares before I focused in on their questions or statements.

Withdrawing is another important and all-too-familiar issue that any depressed person wrestles with. Withdrawing from family and other close-knit social gatherings is usually the most dominant sign of melancholy depression. This can happen extremely early in a person's life. Again, I'm not a therapist; I've lived it and know the signs from the inside out. I agree with what June Hunt says on page 101 in her book *How to Handle Your Emotions*: "Depression is anger drawn within."

Today, we can read accurate, detailed descriptions about emotional illnesses on many reputable websites. One I often turn to is the Mayo Clinic web page. However, no matter how solid the information we read in the privacy of our own homes is, we cannot truly diagnose and give ourselves the one-on-one counseling that we may need to heal mental and emotional issues. If I broke one of my bones, I would see a doctor, so why not visit a therapist about mental and emotional issues?

Personality Disorder

Too often, we accept our own less-than-desirable behavior as unchangeable. Sometimes we'd rather be our own worst enemies than change our behavior. Or perhaps we think we're the normal ones and that everyone else needs therapy. Personality disorders keep many good folks hovering at the edge of normalcy; then, out of the blue, odd behavior, hateful talk, disassociated relationships, constant bad attitudes, addictions, persistent rambling, or more will kick in. (Obviously, I'm referring to more than one person and more than one kind of personality disorder.)

A clear example of this was some information that my mother shared with me. I only mention it here because of its importance to my own story. In 1974, my dad had a major heart attack while driving to Myrtle Beach with my mom. He was driving their first big RV on I-20 near Florence, South Carolina. Even in her eighties, Mom could still recall with sharp detail how she had to take over the steering wheel, pull off the road immediately, and get help quickly.

When they got back to their home here in the Smokies, Dad had to stay put more than usual in order to recover from the heart attack. It was wintertime, so he could barely leave the house; much less drive them both in their RV down to Florida, where they had spent the last few winters. While he was convalescing, he went through a time of depression and anger.

Mom must have had enough of his complaining and griping that winter, so she took Dad to see a psychiatrist. She took him to two sessions; there's no way he would have gone by himself.

During the second session, the doctor pronounced his

diagnosis: Dad has a diagnosed personality disorder! Finally, there was an explanation for Dad's difficult, self-absorbed, addictive personality.

Mom told me that Dad threw his hands up in the air and stomped out screaming that he wasn't crazy. The truth is that no one called him crazy. Having a personality disorder does not mean the person afflicted is crazy or insane in any way.

Being told of Dad's personality diagnosis has given me an explanation for and a sense of closure about all the hateful comments he has made to me throughout my life, not just my childhood. I could never count on my Mom to protect me from his critical, negative words when I was a child; actually, none of us could, and it was a good day when she didn't join in with her own verbal abuse. Usually, when Dad criticized any of us kids, Mom simply treated his words as the gospel truth. We were left to live with the latest outrageous pronouncements that he randomly tossed out at us.

I am not saying that my parents never loved us; they did. However, they rarely expressed their love in understandable terms. In my early adulthood, I was already suffering from melancholy so frequently and severely that I became a poor problem solver and could barely stay employed. All my parents ever said to me about it was, "What's wrong with you? You had a good childhood."

Personality Disorders Do Exist

What is a personality disorder? I'm not qualified to go in depth; however, I will simply say that it is out-of-character behavior compared with who the person is most of the time. The four main forms of such a disorder are narcissistic, schizoid, antisocial, and bipolar. There is also a personality disorder known as borderline personality disorder (BPD). Each disorder has behavior patterns that range from mild to moderate to extreme. Don't think that black-and-white contrasts exist within personality disorders.

Personalities do not come in gift-wrapped boxes with easy-to-understand instructions! We are all inwardly complex beings given to shifting our lives' directions with insight that may have just come our way in a brief amount of time. Think not? One common example of this is a person who accepts Christ as his or her Savior and Lord. Such a change can put that person on a new path that he or she may have never thought of prior to. At least the potential of a new direction is there.

What are the signs of a personality disorder? It would be better for you to go to the Mayo Clinic website and read for yourself. Some common, everyday symptoms are outbursts of anger, social isolation, love-hate relationships, and disconnected and confusing conversations. Unfortunately, people who have such disorders often think they are the most sensible-sounding people.

If you have a difficult home life and you believe it is negatively affecting you, the best action to take is to see a therapist yourself. At the very least, don't try to fix others. This protects your emotions from being damaged and you from carrying that heavy load of stress around.

Accept the Truth

If you even think that you have a personality disorder, first seek out a good therapist to guide you into healing. Please stop ruining others' lives with the dysfunctional outpouring of your disorder. If two or more people have said similar things to you about your personality problems, then, beloved, they are likely right and you likely do have a distorted view of yourself and your world. Distorted views are fixable, though!

If you tend to push others away with an edgy, defensive attitude, you likely have a deeper problem than your loved ones can fix. If you wall yourself up and ignore your loved ones, then I can personally attest that you are in need of a deep inner healing in your psyche.

Ignoring the truth will not make any problem go away, especially psychological ones! If you have a personality disorder, ignoring it may even eventually make you homeless! Homeless people are so beaten down as the result of too many bad choices and short-sighted decisions. My heart goes out to the homeless. Nevertheless, accept the truth of what one or two therapists or close friends have told you about yourself so that you can get on with your healing. The quicker, the better, too!

My Reality Needed Changing

Whatever feelings or opinions my parents had of me at my birth became the unchanging attitudes they have always had toward me. If a child is not wanted in the beginning, then she or he is never wanted. It sounds harsh, but that was apparently my parents' attitude toward me, and I've heard it said many times in group counseling. My parents played different favorites, never treating the five of us in the same way. Realizing these truths has been extremely important to me in my healing. Now I see what I should have seen much earlier in my life.

I kept hoping that they would say how much they loved me or any of those other important statements children, even as adults need to hear from their parents. What I needed to do was change my paradigm regarding who I wanted my parents to be and to accept them for who they really were and are. That took a reality check that came about through several counseling sessions.

Therapy has helped me to change my views of my husband and my extended family and see each one as they really are without having to make them into who I want them to be. This keeps me from being vulnerable to being wounded. If I had had this knowledge in my twenties, I surely would have understood how to love each of them without letting them affect me as they have.

I looked to my family for acceptance and validation, which is logical. However, we all have our flaws. Angry people rarely validate others. Don't seek out an angry person's opinion on something that is controversial. That opens a gate for negative dialogue. That realization has helped me to turn around unproductive communication habits I was not aware I had. With knowledge, I can more easily forgive, also.

I don't spend my time here on earth playing the blame game. Confronting, forgiving, and releasing (letting go and letting God take care of it through prayer and meditation on His Word) is the best formula I've come up with; it works for me. I believe it will work for you, the "wounded one," too.

Meridian Counseling Center

April 2008 was a time of change for me. My paradigm of what love was about had shifted: instead of accepting whatever behavior my loved ones showed to me, I realized that I needed to draw a line of tolerance. I made 2008 my year for possessing good emotional health and went about ensuring that that line stuck.

For long periods of my life, I have been loved almost into an early grave—or perhaps emotional breakdown—by various family members who couldn't see that what they were saying to me was all that harmful. Family members can be hurtful in how they release their pent-up anger to ones they love the most. Obviously, I struggled with making it clear just how much I was being pushed to the edge. I needed a therapist to guide me into good emotional health. We can't always count on love not to have some hurt wrapped up in it.

That April, I walked through the doors at Meridian Behavioral Health Center, a local mental health provider in my area, for the first time. I immediately liked their approach to teaching good mental health skills and knew that this was a place where I needed to be. Meridian is not a "lock-up" facility but a place where both group classes and individual counseling are given. Students come and go freely.

It was at Meridian that the psychologist finally put her finger on my problem: dysthymic depression. I finally had an answer for my chronic mood swings and withdrawal into times of solitary pensiveness. Knowing that made me face my problem and deal with it.

I completed several of Meridian's self-help programs and also went through some one-on-one counseling. It was my own decision to attend their programs. Jeff was gone through the week and with only my poodle at home, I had plenty of time to let what I learned there soak in.

I had done so well in the classes that the mental health team invited me to attend their very intensive peer-counseling leadership classes for the Wellness Recovery Action Plan, or WRAP, classes. I'm glad to this day that I took them up on that offer. I graduated from all the courses I took with a new sense of resolve not to carry around the background baggage that I had spent decades dragging around and adding to.

Most important for me is that I learned how not to set myself up for failure by playing the victim card, which I did by carrying around depression fueled by unresolved anger, leading to a self-defeated attitude. I also learned to minimize my tendency to be a fixer, which has often set me up for hurt. At Meridian, I realized that I can't make other people happy; each person's feelings are the result of that person's own inward decision. It is not my responsibility to change someone else's attitude. Instead, I need to take time for me and not let myself become emotionally drained by living to please others or seeking their validation.

Prior to Meridian, I had occasionally gone to a therapist, even yelling at that empty chair I mentioned earlier. But those early attempts at counseling never seemed to get to my real problem, which was undiagnosed depression.

My experience at Meridian was both positive and supportive. I felt really good about what I was learning. I believed in myself more than I ever had before. I remember attending the first few WRAP classes and thinking, *I am going to attend a year of their programs.* And I did! I went for a few hours one evening each week during that year. For the first eight weeks, I also had one-on-one peer counseling for about an hour prior to attending the WRAP sessions.

The WRAP program was developed by Mary Ellen Copeland, PhD. Each program has twelve lesson plans, and a teen-tailored program is available as well. Copeland saw the need for WRAP after experiencing her own mental health crisis. Her foundation is dedicated to mental health issues, and information about it can be found on the Internet.

Seeking Truth Brings Peace

There is no solving anything in our individual lives until self-honesty consumes us. Truth about each of us needs to be exposed to our searching hearts. Then, and only then, we can have the peace that surpasses all understanding (Phil. 4:7).

Sometimes we think there is only one type of truth: our own version. Sometimes our version of truth really is the same as actual truth. We find truth when we are honest with ourselves and start earnestly searching for it. However, there has always been a sly version of the truth that's usually very believable. In Genesis 3:1, the serpent shaped a half-truth of what God had earlier spoken to Adam and Eve, and it's been that way ever since.

When I began going to counseling sessions, I finally had to admit the truth that I was a depressed person and that I had lived most of my life being that way. My version of the truth just hadn't worked out to be the real truth. I thought that being healed of depression meant getting off drugs, becoming a Christian, marrying a good Christian man, raising good children (and they are, thank God), attending church, graduating from college, and even balancing the checkbook.

All of those actions did help me to get above the smog level of deep depression, but none proved to be the cure I truly needed. What I needed to do was to admit the real truth that I had too big of an emotional problem to be resolved by the usual life activities. Neither could my husband solve my most inner turmoil. Jeff had no knowledge on how to solve even his own emotional problems; it wasn't right for either of us to take our stress and anxieties out on our young children, either.

I needed professional counseling to solve my issues, and it was time for me to admit it instead of denying it. When I faced that truth and started taking those first baby steps that led me to the WRAP program—and later to the Wise Mind group and the one-on-one peer counseling sessions—then I truly began to be healed.

Every now and then I still attend counseling because I am determined that I will not spend another moment of my life carrying the heavy emotions of unresolved turmoil around anymore.

My favorite Bible verse is "Give all your worries and cares to God, for he cares about you." 1 Peter 5:7 (NLT 2nd ed). I had this verse reference put on my license plate because I want everyone who is behind my vehicle to know that they don't have to carry any burden by themselves because God is always there for them. I get asked about it often and am able to tell believers and nonbelievers alike about the freedom I've found in claiming that verse.

4 Fs

In May 1976, I enlisted in the US Air Force, and during my four-year enlistment, I earned a Good Conduct Medal. At the end of my service, I received an honorable discharge. All in all, it was time well spent. But these four *Fs* aren't related to those commonly referred to in the military.

These four *F*'s relate to the whole of my life. At Meridian, I first thought about summing up my experiences in life as "4 F." I even used that as the title for my presentation to the peer-leadership class. "4 F" stands for "failure, faith, family, and freedom."

During the year I spent receiving counseling at Meridian, I learned not to share family "war stories." However, I'm going to depart from that sound advice in order for the reader to understand (and maybe relate to) my particular journey through and out of chronic melancholy depression.

By the time I graduated high school, I was already wrestling with deep-seated feelings of failure and aimlessness. I made no plans because I didn't believe that I would be able to accomplish any of them. Neither of my parents ever really had a positive attitude toward me. As a matter of fact, in my childhood and even in my adult years, it was a good day when neither parent focused on me because their dialogue quickly became both negative and critical.

Throughout my childhood, Dad would look straight at me, point his finger, and say, "Kiddo, you're just not pretty enough" or "tall enough," "You're too fat" (I was an overweight child, but being criticized about it never helped), "Your teeth are too crooked" (they were, but my parents refused to have them straightened; I did decades later), or some other negative statement that let me know that I was never going to measure up to his unreachable standards. It's an odd fact, but my dad spent many of his adult years being about as round as he is tall! He took what he didn't like about himself out on me and my siblings. Learning not to take ownership of Dad's and Mom's criticisms of me over issues that were beyond my ability to correct would come much later in my life through counseling sessions.

I do believe that Dad subconsciously transferred what he didn't like about himself onto each of his children by constantly criticizing any or all of us. He never has liked taking the blame for his own wrongful decisions and has always tried to blame us or take his anger out on us in some way.

Unexpected Closure for Me

Several weeks after I had quit working for my parents, I went back to their business to tidy up my account there. While working at their warehouse, I had purchased several items on credit to sell on eBay. In an awkward moment, my parents asked why I was seeing a therapist. In their minds, I had experienced a near-perfect childhood, so they were near demanding in knowing why I even thought that I might have an emotional problem.

I had never told them that I was going to group counseling at Meridian, nor had I ever criticized them about their parenting. I usually don't express my inner thoughts if I perceive that doing so will bring about conflict. And, frankly, I don't see the purpose in stating my every thought anyway. I am not a "gabber."

Nevertheless, when Mom lived by herself, I made sure that I ate supper with her at least once a week during the last several years of her life, and Jeff occasionally went over to visit her as well. I made sure that my mother saw her great-grandchildren when my daughter Rachel came to visit us. (Mom had already passed when Rachel moved nearer to us.) Besides that, I have always lived my own quiet life. It's in my alone time that I can regroup and get my perspective in focus.

My parents lived some fifteen miles from me at the time I had this warehouse encounter, so I didn't see either of them every day. And I did happen to be in my fifties and felt I had a perfect right to make up my mind on how I wanted to spend my time here on earth. I couldn't figure out why these two elderly people felt they needed to know what they didn't need to know, or at least so I thought. God, however, had another opinion of the situation.

This moment in their warehouse proved to be the only

moment of closure I would ever have with either of my parents. It was not of my choosing, but they had cornered me. All I can say is that the Spirit of God opened my mouth, and I relayed to them in complete detail the most severe moment of their parenting of me.

I reminded my parents that neither one of them let us girls defend ourselves, nor did they protect us from our brothers' anger. That didn't satisfy them, so I described the broken window incident, when Dad had whipped me. I described details of the color of the couch and carpet. I was even able to describe the smell of pinto beans simmering on the stove, with Mom standing to my left. Then I looked at my parents. My mother turned away from me, about to cry, and my dad threw his hands up in the air, blaming my mom for making him a parent! I left immediately afterward.

Solutions to Loving Difficult People

If someone you know is your constant critic, especially if they are elderly, accept the fact that they will not change. The best idea is to stop reacting to every hurtful word spoken to you. You will only get into an argument with them if you react. Try to let most of what is said go in one ear and out the other.

To my regret, I did not visit my mother very much during her last few weeks on earth because her ever-increasing criticisms of our family members grew to be too much for my nerves. My sister, Deena and her husband Jude lived with her at that time, so I knew she was well taken care of. However, I regret that I was focused on my own wounds at that time. Mom was dying of cancer but did not let any of us know that until her emergency room visit around Thanksgiving 2009.

When my parents separated a few years earlier, I did spend time with Mom on a weekly basis until my sister moved in with her, and then I slacked off. When I visited, I helped her cook and we ate supper together. We watched TV or worked in her flower beds after supper. During those evenings, I just let Mom tell me whatever she wanted to. Our worlds were far apart in many ways. Prior to therapy, it was just a good day when I felt that I could leave my home. Mom, on the other hand, ran a business and was well known throughout the Great Smoky Mountain tourist areas. My visits usually worked out okay, but all of our relatives sure got a severe tongue-lashing behind their backs during those visits.

Improving My Physical Health and Managing RA

When I quit nursing my oldest child Ruth, I began having some severe joint aches. I was about twenty-nine at that time. A military doctor did some blood work on me and came back with the diagnosis of rheumatoid arthritis.

During my three pregnancies and while I was nursing my three children during each of their first year, I was nearly as healthy as they were. I wasn't seriously bothered by RA until after my third child was weaned. That's when I began feeling the aches coming back to my joints. Fortunately, God has always given me fairly good health and a lot of stamina. I have pretty much always been able to keep up with my daughters—and now my grandchildren too!

I have taken prescription NSAIDs (non-steroidal anti-inflammatory drugs) for over twenty years, along with other drugs my doctors ordered up. For about ten years, I took Remicade infusions, which I tolerated well, about every eight weeks. However, one day I decided to march to the beat of a different drum.

Jeff and I had been getting vitamins from a local health food store, so one day I asked the herbalist how he might be able to help me control my RA. He put me on a cleansing kit for two weeks and then gave me about a two-hour consultation. In a few days, he had an herbal compound for me that he had mixed and put into capsules. I was to take two three times a day. I've been doing that for over two years now, have taken no prescriptions or infusions during that time, and show no signs of aggression in my RA.

My rheumatologist, Dr. Kristen Gowin of Asheville Arthritis Practice, has been impressed with my lack of swelling and still maintaining good agility. I follow her recommendation to take calcium daily. For years, I took an over-the-counter calcium pill and still experienced bone density loss. It turns out that calcium comes from a lot of different sources—some we absorb and some we don't.

When I went to the herbalist, I found a powder mix of calcium, vitamin D3, and magnesium that I've been taking for some time now. I mix a scoop of it with a glass of tepid lemon water three times a day, giving me a total of 1,500 units of calcium gluconate, which works best for me.

The magnesium and vitamin D3 that are included in the mix also help me keep a more upbeat mood. Another natural mood booster is 5-HTP, a natural replacement for serotonin. I take 5-HTP to replace the serotonin that I'm losing because I'm over fifty. During the winter I take a lot of extra vitamin C and D since I'm more indoors.

I believe one reason that I'm still agile is because I've taken a tablespoon of cod liver oil along with some orange juice most nights for over twenty years. The extra benefit of fish oil is more vitamin D getting into my system. I've kept common viruses at bay by taking one or two tablespoons of *Bragg's Apple Cider Vinegar* a day (doing this keeps my immune system alkaline). At Dr. Gowin's suggestion, I have added strontium for building bone density. I'm frequently researching what else I can be doing to help improve my health and keep an open mind to new ideas. I frequently watch *Know the Cause*, and/or *Dr. Oz*.

Over my lifetime, I have had many stress-related illnesses, sometimes termed psychosomatic illnesses. In my teen years, I sometimes had flare-ups of a gum disease, but I solved that by having a tooth removed in my twenties. About two years after I joined the Air Force, an observant dentist noticed my receding gum line. He grafted some skin from the roof of my mouth onto my gum line, and that's why I still have my natural teeth to this day.

In my early forties, uterine cancer showed up on my yearly pap smear. Fortunately, it was in the beginning stages and surgery solved it. Since then, I've had outbreaks of psoriasis, which my family physician says is, of course, a stress-related condition. Furthermore, I've had gout (also stress related) and migraines (absolutely stress related).

Because of RA, I've had surgeries to remove inflamed joints and to correct hammertoes on each of my feet. The final surgery was done to take out a metal shank in my toe that my body had decided to reject six months after my foot surgery.

I'm not against antidepressants, but I have never taken any. Instead, I have learned to let go of any negative message that has been spoken to me. I don't wear others' poor attitudes like I used to. I don't smoke or drink alcoholic beverages, nor do I consciously do anything that would cause depression to be inflamed.

Most important, I don't allow people to make comments about poor health to me. At least some of what afflicts us can be held at bay by maintaining a positive attitude.

The Valley of Trouble, the Door of Hope

In the fall of 2009, I visited my minister, Rev. Rich Peoples, because I was experiencing high levels of anxiety related to unresolved issues in my life, both past and present. Before leaving my house, I felt a headache coming on, but, being in a rush, I didn't take time to wash down a few aspirin, which I was regretting by the time I arrived. Nevertheless, I insisted that we press on with our meeting. As we stepped into his office, I looked out at the afternoon autumn sun that was streaming in through some tall, rectangular windows.

When Pastor Rich had set our appointment, he stated that he was more of a minister than a counselor. Nevertheless, he guided me through a valley of trouble and into a "door of hope" (Hosea 2:15). This happened simply because I reached out and found a "trained guide" who guided me through that dark valley.

My hour-long appointment lasted one and half hours. As we closed in prayer, I felt a huge sense of relief wash over me. My headache, however, had turned into a piercing migraine. The harsh sunlight was creeping ever closer to me on its afternoon journey. I made the ten miles back home on prayer, sheer determination, and a renewed sense of joy!

The Door, the Key

Every sane person has at least one blind spot; therefore, every married couple has at least one blind gap. One day, I saw one of my children stumble toward her dad's and my blind gap. That was the day my healing started. That was the day the school guidance counselor called me to suggest family counseling; and I said yes, we would pursue that.

When I was young, I was not so much aware that there was a devious spirit force known as Satan that was seeking to destroy me, and anyone else for that matter. It seemed to me that there was plenty right at hand to be afraid of. Since my youth, however, I've come to understand that any one of us can fall prey to being our own worst enemy. We often glibly glide along in a world of our own choosing, not realizing that we're heading into a descent of our own making.

Even for one person to fall prey to his own worst ideas is bad enough, but in truth, we are a microcosm of humanity, and one person's bad idea affects multiple people, just like a good idea does. That's why I'm still glad we attended those early counseling sessions.

Boundaries by Drs. Townsend and Cloud

During Jeff's convalescing time after experiencing his atrial fibrillation, he and I began attending Boundaries sessions. We attended all nine sessions together and really got a lot out of the classes. *Boundaries* are a series of DVD sessions plus a workbook that was written by Drs. Henry Cloud and John Townsend.

Boundaries include a series of teachings on how to better communicate with people in our lives. Each session is filled with well-explained teachings that interconnect with the last DVD session and then take the participant into new territory on how to take better control of our individual lives.

Both authors are Christian men. Jeff and I attended a weeknight small-group gathering that was hosted by Elizabeth Dewees of Christ-Centered Counseling at her church, which is near Sylva. *Boundaries* makes for a great choice as an alternative Sunday evening class, and attending Elizabeth's small group became one of Jeff's and my couple outings.

What I've Learned through Counseling and My Own Seeking

The keys for me in finding good mental and emotional health have been being honest with myself and attending the different types of counseling I've discussed. Listed below are the highlights of what I've learned:

- **Build your self-respect.** Be involved in mentally and emotionally healthy involvements that build your character and self-esteem. Avoid self-centered involvements that may feel good for a season but usually have a sad harvest connected to them.

- **Those who wound the deepest are the least likely people to validate anyone but themselves.** These people are usually manipulative in their friendships with others ("I'm in it for what you can do for me").

- **Be your own agent of change.** Be in charge of your own healing! Seek out trustworthy counselors who don't just label you with a disorder and then sound like a broken record thereafter. Find one who can help you move beyond the label and into the healing.

- Also don't count on loved ones to heal you. Family members are rarely qualified to hand out in-depth counseling. And even if they are, like my daughter Ruth, who is a licensed therapist, they are too intertwined in the family to give the best advice. That almost always divides a family because of personal knowledge. Please seek counsel from trusted professionals. It is not God's will for you to suffer with unresolved emotional issues.

- **Don't expect closure from those who have wounded you.** You may get closure in some unexpected way, but don't let that be a requirement for your healing. Don't keep expecting the people who have wounded you to behave outside of their standard pattern of behavior. In the meantime, your life is moving on and you need to catch up with it!

- **Be thankful and show thankfulness when progress has been made.** I'm grateful that Jeff willingly attended counseling with me. A counselor can sort out the issues in couple communication and more readily see the communication patterns. Counseling was so stress relieving for Jeff that he actually sought out his own counselor. Having experienced atrial fibrillation, he realized he was carrying around too much stress and unresolved anger that was silently affecting his health.

- **Know your personal limits of what you can take emotionally.** I had to go to counseling to understand that. I had unwittingly let others' negative issues pile on top of me through the decades. You must change the way you communicate with those who have wounded you. You are the one who needs to set your own boundaries!

- **The power grabbers keep wounding the wounded in order to keep the power!** When God planted that phrase in my mind, I couldn't wait to write it down! Don't hand your power over. Tell yourself that you respect yourself too much to do that. Tell others, "I love you too much to argue with you" and walk away.

- **Don't own the wounds others have spoken over you.** An example of this is when I was a child and my dad criticized me for my crooked teeth and my chubbiness. I became a victim of low self-esteem and stinking thinking about myself. Those pronouncements created plenty of problems, but what problems were solved? None. It took counseling, therapy, and prayer to disown others' pronouncements over me.

- **Own the real problem so you can solve it.** Take charge of your healing. In my late thirties, I owned up to my crooked teeth and sought the care of an excellent orthodontist in Sumter. We had just rotated back to the States, and getting my teeth straightened became a priority of mine. The orthodontist not only corrected my teeth but also, for free, made an appliance to stop and correct one of my daughters' thumb-sucking habit and in general corrected many future dental problems all three girls were at the verge of developing.

- **Respect yourself and find time for your own interests.** I gave and gave until I was empty, and then I got filled up with others' hurtful criticisms of me, which nearly broke my emotional health. My parents struggled with how to teach the five of us how to respect one another. I've struggled with self-respect throughout my life. I believe I'm here today because God sent angels unawares to minister to me during my deepest depressed times (Heb. 13:2).

- **Believe in yourself.** One thing I did for myself while we lived in Sumter was to attend and graduate from college. It had been a dream of mine since high school, and I made it my time to fulfill that dream. It was tough, though. I failed three of four math courses I had to take. It took me five and half years to complete my degree requirements, but I enjoyed the liberal arts atmosphere. One thing that kept me going was that I envisioned myself walking across the stage holding my diploma and saying to myself, "I fulfilled this dream!"

I enjoyed getting out of the house and being introduced to new ideas and subjects that I never would have thought of on my own. Being much older and more rooted in my beliefs than the average college student, I easily retained my conservatism and Christian beliefs. I graduated Coker College with a Bachelor's of Arts in Sociology in 2000.

- **Don't expect others to heal you.** Your healing comes from within you. Your confidant or whomever you count on to pull you up out of the dumps is likely an untrained "coach." It's often hard work to get true peace, but it's always well worth the effort. Seek out a Christian therapist, if at all possible. A licensed counselor or therapist is there to help you face your problems and guide you into healing.

- **Controllers control!** They're not going to behave any other way. I avoid controllers because they end up pushing me farther into depression. Like most people, I don't want to be controlled. It seems reasonable to me. God did give me a very able mind. I don't see everything, and that's why I seek counsel, not control.

- **Don't try to fix others' wrongful attitudes.** It has taken therapy for me to break my "fixer" response to others' problems. No one really has the power to change someone else's personality. That kind of healing comes from within.

- **Stop generational anger.** I've always shown my elders respect, as I was taught to. The disrespect that my parents, family, and in-laws showed me has always stopped with me; otherwise, I would have played a part in continuing the cycle of anger.

- **Prescriptions for depression are okay.** I'm not against prescriptions for depression, and I wish that some of the lighter ones I see advertised on TV had been around a few decades back. Nevertheless, prescribed medications to help overcome depression or to limit anger are best for a limited time only.

- Therapy, counseling, and owning up to the truth that depression or unresolved anger is the "monkey on your back" are the best paths to take for healing. And especially don't discount the simple idea of picking up a pen and writing whatever crazy thought that comes to you on paper. After all, that's exactly what I've done here!

- **Get help if you have addictions.** Alcohol and drugs make for poor listeners. People with addiction issues need both counseling and a support group. I have no known addictions, and I am grateful that neither Jeff nor our daughters have any drug issues and only drink moderately, if at all.

    I do know and respect a retired medical doctor in my church who has worked in the addiction-counseling field for more than thirty years. His name is Dr. Winn Henderson. Through his medical practice, he developed a successful addictions program and has written a book titled *Freedom from Addictions*. It can be found on the Internet.

This kind (of demon) will only come out by prayer and fasting. (Matt. 17:21 NAS)

- **Maintain a routine.** This one has never been a problem for me. I've always gotten up early, stayed up late, and kept a full day in between. I've never been one to stay in bed late or even take a nap during the day. However, so many people I've listened to in group counseling do have problems maintaining a routine.

    Find some solid reason for maintaining an effective routine. The best way is to say to yourself, "I love myself too much to not give myself the best chance to succeed today. Today is my time! Today is my time to get out for a walk and to connect with people on a positive basis!"

- **Forgive.** Life is too short not to! Forgive yourself where needed. Also do your best to forgive those who have treated you wrongly. Then let go of your negative emotions. I've been able to completely forgive through prayer, Bible reading, attending counseling sessions, and journaling. It's been very freeing for me to forgive. And forgiving has probably added good health and years to my life!

    Forgiveness does not excuse poor, disrespectful behavior, but it does allow you to move on. You have your own life to live to its fullest! It might take therapy for you to start forgiving, but that's okay.

"When you were dead in your transgressions ... He made you alive together with Him, having forgiven us all our transgressions, having cancelled out the certificate of debt ... having nailed it to the cross." (Col. 2: 13–14 NAS)

- **Accept the fact that life is sometimes unfair.** No, I didn't have to go to counseling to learn this one. Counseling just helped me to straighten out the unfair part. Once you bring this truth into your consciousness, then go about making your life fair by seeking counseling if needed and forgive others who have wronged you. Do your best to not participate in others' whining, arguing, criticizing, gossiping, or any other ungodly behavior toward others. Seek out the best solutions to life's problems by seeking wisdom primarily through a deepening understanding of God. (Prov. 1:7)

- **Exercise!** Studies show that exercise improves our overall physical health and mental-emotional health.

- **Plant a Flower garden!** Or find some other hobby or craft to indulge in that helps you to put your mind on pleasant things. My mother's Zinnia garden ringed around a tall white bird bath and was a front yard "show stopper!" All the neighbors really enjoyed going by her house from spring to late fall with her brick house lined with blazing azaleas, blooming rhododendron, and weeping cherry tree. She grew marigolds as tall as me in her backyard and had many other plants and planted a yearly small vegetable garden also. Since moving into our house I've taken up flower gardening as well!

A Vision God Gave to Me

I received a vision while I was driving to work on the Cherokee Indian reservation, where I was a sales clerk at one of the gift shops in the summer of 2010. I was leaving Sylva and had just gone under the US 441 South viaduct that heads toward Franklin and then on to Atlanta, Georgia. It's barely one eighth of a mile from that overpass to Victory Baptist Church, which has always been a prayer corridor for me. This vision happened within that eighth of a mile.

Just as I passed under the bridge, it seemed as though I were no longer driving my Explorer. I saw myself being let out of a jail cell that was at the end of a long corridor. As I passed the other cells that were filled with screaming, writhing inmates I noticed something odd about each of the cells. When I got to the exit door, I stopped briefly and asked the guard, "When did they remove the cell doors?" He clearly told me that there had never been any doors. Any of us could leave any time we wanted to! With that, I stepped out into the softest white light that could ever exist.

I believe the interpretation of that vision is that we stay in bondage because we don't make seeking freedom our priority. At some point in each of our lives, we need to decide whether to live life as a victim or a victor.

Your Miracle Is at Hand!

Sometimes, my loved ones think I'm in charge of the local complaint department. I'll admit that my "Sure, I'll listen" attitude sometimes places me squarely in that chair even if I'm simply doing my best to mind my own business. With cell phones being all too handy, we really can reach out and touch someone about anytime anyone of us takes a notion to.

I'm not really in charge of complaints, nor am I in charge of criticisms, but both seem to slip in some days no matter what. There are those who seem determined to get the last word in or complain about something with every breath they take. We all have at least one family member, but likely a few, who has a difficult personality. And by no means am I suggesting that we should love them any less than we do the more lovable ones.

Drawing the line on unacceptable attitudes and behavior with our loved ones is difficult. I'm not a therapist, but I have finally experienced a breakthrough on this subject partly through prayer and meditation on Scripture. Though this is strictly my own insight into this following Biblical account, I hope I convey to you how I have rid my thoughts of others' negative messages that used to burden me.

The Bible tells of two miracles concerning an increase in what was desperately needed in two widows' homes. (What do you and I need?) The first is in 1 Kings 17: 10–16, and the second one, the one I want to focus on, is in 2 Kings 4:1–7. Since it's lengthy, please read it in your Bible. In the conversation in verses 1 and 2, we read that the woman knew that Elisha was a man of God. I believe her to be a devout Jew, which is why she knew him. She likely knew God through what her husband had taught his family; he had been a servant of Elisha and a son of a prophet.

Now, though, she was widowed and had exhausted her means in providing for her family. She was at the end of herself. She needed a miracle, and Elisha was her "point of contact" with Yahweh. Through Elisha, she experienced her miracle.

During the thirteen years we lived in Sumter, South Carolina, I was active in church, doing bulletin boards and organizing at least one pictorial directory. Well, at least that was the outer me that everyone saw. I didn't participate in Sunday school and made it to church only on a somewhat regular basis. I talked to very few people and actually had few friends, period. I was suffering from that general, unfocused malaise about things—my then-undiagnosed dysthymic depression—and had been for too many years to count.

I often saw my minister, Rev. Victor Cheek, but would say no more than a greeting or small talk. I could have made him my "point of contact" and confided in him about my troubles, both current and past, but I did not. I was raised not to "wear my feelings on my sleeves;" plus, my parents didn't put up with a whiner or complainer attitude from any of us kids. There is a lot of good in those teachings; however, my role model, my mother—who had plenty to cry about regarding her marriage to my dad—rarely, if ever, wept or complained about his obvious shortcomings. My dad loves us all but was often a "bull in a china shop" when it came to family life.

In 2009 I began to finally come to the end of myself. By this time, Jeff and I had been living in Sylva, North Carolina, and had become charter members of Grace Community Church. We both had gotten to know our minister, Dr. Rich Peoples, fairly well. After all it was Rich's conservative, contemporary style of teaching that led us to join him and several others in forming Grace Community Church.

It was on an early fall day in 2009 that I confided in Rich, telling him about the many issues I had never really faced. It was like "cleansing my earthly vessel" so the "oil of joy" (Ps. 45:7b) could be poured in. I have been experiencing my miraculous overflow of joy and connective attitude ever since!

God is patiently waiting for you to get to the "end of yourself" so you can find a point of godly contact in order to receive the miracle he has for you.

Some Laws Should Never Be Broken

There are laws that govern our psyches that should never be broken. Perhaps you, like I, have subconsciously lived with the negative results of a generational personality disorder. One day I realized that my own pattern of behavior was keeping me from reaching goals I had consciously planned for myself. You also may have been wounded repeatedly by others in your life, and the anger over it is keeping you from living in joy. There is good news—you can break those negative thought cycles that are holding you down!

Through therapy, a willingness to be honest with myself, and deep soul-searching, I have broken patterns of self-defeating speech that have improved my relationship with my husband and all my other family members as well.

You can never weed out all the difficult people in your life. We are not islands; we all need others to be involved with on several levels. The important thing is to stop reacting to others' negativity and start living out your action plan for a positive life. Believe and live as if your healing has already taken place!

The day you forgive and let go of the hurts in your life is the day you walk into the newness of life. That's the day your emotional healing happens. Don't sit on the sidelines of life one more minute. Your life is waiting for you; begin living it to the fullest starting today.

Watch Out for the Trapdoor!

Have you ever noticed someone who you thought had it all together suddenly start doing something so out of character that you wonder if body snatchers have come and put someone new into his/her skin? Perhaps, for some reason, your loved one or friend has fallen through the trapdoor of their emotions that leads to some level of emotional disarray. Would that resolve it for you? Even though you want to, you probably can't truly help them. The best you can do is to not let them pull you down too.

What makes the trapdoor of our emotions fall open? Did we forget to lock the hasp the last time we got pulled out from that dark place? If I'm describing you, you're the only one who can answer these questions. You are your own expert on how you feel!

Always be honest with yourself. Don't trust your own judgment all the time; you just might be the one who is steering yourself in the wrong direction. Ask God to send a few trustworthy, wise people your way to give advice you can trust. Seek out trusted elders in your Christian fellowship and spend time listening to them. Perhaps you can help them with some task while you soak up their wisdom.

Sports stars have personal trainers and our president has advisors; why shouldn't we seek input from a few trusted individuals for some of our problems? Just make sure it's the best advice you can find for yourself. You only get to live your life once!

Three Different Time Zones

> This is the day the Lord has made;
> We will rejoice and be glad in it.
> (Ps. 118:24)

We all tend to live in three different time zones:
1. Any day now, I'm gonna
2. Someday, I'm know I'm gonna
3. Today, I will ...

It took many years, but eventually, I told myself, "Today, I will draw a line in the shifting sands of my time here on earth and change what must change if I don't want my past mistakes to be my future problems!"

When I decided to go to counseling, I literally broke a lifestyle trend that had made me falsely convinced that I could fix everyone's problems. I'm doing good to keep myself organized! I knew something had to change, but it took spending time with a counselor to put in place the "today" commitment I had made to myself. I knew that if I didn't make a more outward decision right then, my weaknesses would once again be my tomorrows' downfalls.

I actually believe that I subconsciously willed myself to change because I spent the first half of 2008 being very miserable. Then, in April of that year, two things happened that changed the course of both Jeff's and my lives. The first, as I mentioned, was that I realized my view of life was getting out of focus. It's hard to describe—I wasn't losing my sanity, but I began a more significant descent into functioning depression. Perhaps autopilot living describes it best. I began listening to my family's opinion that something just wasn't "gelling" in my thinking and finally decided that they couldn't all be wrong while I'm right.

I'm not one to play the odds, so finally the reality of where I was headed if I didn't change course became clear to me.

At about that same time, Jeff, without my knowing it spent a serious amount of time in prayer, some for me but also for God to lead us to a church home. We had moved back to North Carolina a few years earlier but still hadn't found one. As a matter of fact, I had stopped even looking. Within a few days, Rev. Peoples knocked on our door, said he was canvassing the area with a few others, and asked if Jeff would be interested in a short visit then or to simply visit the church he was the pastor of during that time. I wasn't home then, but Jeff told me later how he had unloading on a near perfect stranger. True story! I can't even make something that good up. I'm not that inventive.

Ever so slowly, the "octopus tentacles" that were entangling me began to loosen. We began attending that church, I stayed in counseling, and we bought a house and threw out the proverbial anchor. One of our daughters found herself a career job here in Sylva, the other two have started and are finishing college near us, and our young grandchildren are a part of our lives. Both Jeff and I are more positive minded than we ever had been before. In brief, life just keeps getting better!

Above all else, I pray that you will find your emotional healing through good counseling and also within the safe harbor of Jesus Christ. I hope my book has been helpful to you or your loved one who is experiencing depression.

As I stated in the beginning, I'm not a therapist, a counselor, or a theologian. Nevertheless, I hope my story of hope and healing has in some way helped you on your life's journey.

Contact the Author

I am willing to share more of my healing journey in depth, though I'm certainly not a polished speaker. All I require is a love gift offering to cover my expenses. My most important requirement, however, is that I be allowed to freely talk about my Christian faith and include biblical references with no hindrances.

I can be reached at myjourneyintohealing@hotmail.com or Patricia Jordan, PO Box 766, Sylva, NC 28779.

CPSIA information can be obtained at www.ICGtesting.com
Printed in the USA
LVOW13s0758041013

355331LV00001B/89/P